Wild rivers are earth's renegades, defying gravity, dancing to their own tunes, resisting the authority of humans, always chipping away, and eventually always winning. And wild rivers bring out the renegade in us, enticing us to leave behind all that we've been taught and to let ourselves surrender to their special symphony. When I was in high school, I would climb out of my bedroom window for midnight canoe runs, or say I was at a slumber party when I was off rafting for the weekend. The river was a kindred spirit. I shared a secret with the river, a knowledge that the clearest way into the universe was downstream.

RICHARD BANGS

Kayaking Magic Falls on the Kennebec, west-central Maine.

WHITEWATER ADVENTURE

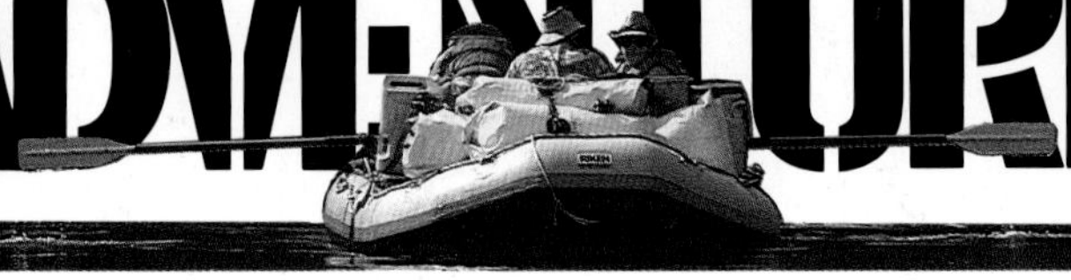

Corkscrew Rapid on the Chattooga, the river made famous in the film Deliverance.

WHITEWATER ADVENTURE

Running America's Great Scenic Rivers

WRITTEN BY RICHARD BANGS
PRODUCED BY McQUISTON & PARTNERS

THUNDER BAY PRESS, SAN DIEGO

We were awkward paddlers and the canoe crankled through the water as though drunk. We bobbed and weaved upstream and slowly picked up some proficiency as we angled toward Difficult Run Rapids marking the end of the gorge. The white-breasted water got faster as we got closer, and my blood accelerated correspondingly. This was exciting! Then we were in the rooster tails of the rapid, being flung up and down on a dizzy aquatic seesaw, paddling with all our strength. "Let's go higher," I screamed over the rapid's roar, and we sunk our blades deeper and lunged forward. Then the bow snapped to the side, abruptly capsizing the canoe and precipitating us into the spume. We'd been christened as river runners.

To Bali and Borneo, and their mom.

At the end of a river trip, at the take-out when the boats are tugged on shore, backs are slapped, arms are wrapped in hugs, and expressions of gratitude are made. This is the take-out for this book, and my chance to back-slap and hug and thank everyone who paddled with me.

First of all, I want to acknowledge Pamela Roberson, who collected much of the photography appearing in these pages. Assisting Pamela were Sloane Smith and Johannes Tan, who also helped with editorial research. Others who helped on the editorial end were Sobek staff members Yanthie Indrakusuma, Jo Anne Coates, Leslie Jarvie, Christine Hult, Tricia Newkirk, Russ Daggatt, and Denise Faria. Jim Cassidy, one of the gurus of rafting, provided invaluable supporting material; Payson Kennedy, John Land, Verne Huser, and Slim Ray generously shared their deep-river knowledge. I am grateful to the original members of The Raft Club: John Yost, Ricky Vierbuchen, Steve Hatleberg, Dave Nurney, and member-in-protest John Kramer, as well as to fellow rafters and friends Breck O'Neill, Bart Henderson, and Rick Szabo. I am also indebted to the following individuals and organizations: Wayne and Suzie Hockmeyer of Northern Outdoors, Mark Mills of Outback Expeditions, Ted and Don Hatch of Hatch River Expeditions, the Canoe Cruisers Association, and Friends of the River.

Mostly, I thank my parents, Louise and Dr. Lawrence Bangs, who put up with my river madness, even supported it when others were naysaying. They drove shuttles, lent car and gas money, and spent many nights awake wondering if I would survive my latest river expedition.
—RICHARD BANGS

Photo Credits:
Front Cover: American River, California by Liz Hymans.
Back Cover: Snake River, Wyoming by Jeff Foott.
Half title page: Bruce Dunn.
Title page: Pamela Roberson.

Whitewater Adventure is our third book for Thunder Bay Press. So again we thank our publishers Charles Tillinghast and Craig Schafer for their continued confidence and support. We also gratefully acknowledge the many fine photographers whose names appear next to their images. On the editorial side, special thanks go to Robin Witkin for her invaluable contribution to the text. Finally, we are indebted to author/river-god Richard Bangs for sharing his rafting experiences that provided so much enjoyment during the production of this book.
—McQUISTON & PARTNERS

Library of Congress Cataloging-in-Publication Data
Bangs, Richard, 1950-
    Whitewater adventure: running America's great scenic rivers/written by Richard Bangs; produced by McQuiston & Partners. p. cm.
    1. Rafting (Sports)—North America. 2. White-water canoeing—North America. 3. North America—Description and travel—1981-I. McQuiston & Partners. II. Title.
GV776.05.B36   1990   917—dc20   89-80491 CIP
ISBN 0-934429-20-0
10 9 8 7 6 5 4 3 2 1

Portions of the essay on the Tatshenshini River first appeared in *Rivergods*, by Richard Bangs and Christian Kallen (Sierra Club Books, 1985), and are used by permission of the publisher.

Printed in Japan by Dai Nippon Printing Co., Ltd.

Published by Thunder Bay Press
5880 Oberlin Drive
San Diego, California 92121

CONTENTS

James Thompson/Rapid Shooters

Great Falls of the Potomac River above Washington, D.C.

BEGINNINGS

I t's a singularly American rite of passage, reading the Mark Twain masterpiece, *Adventures of Huckleberry Finn*. I was a junior at Walt Whitman High School in Bethesda, Maryland, and the story of Huck and Jim and their raft trip down the Mississippi affected me in a way that Jay Gatsby and his silk shirts, or George Babbitt's conformity, or even Natty Bumppo's "noble savage" never would. Huck discovered adventure, beauty, self-reliance, peace, and true human values by rafting down the river. "It's lovely to live on a raft," Huck said, and I believed him. I wanted to raft a river.

I lived just a few miles from the Potomac, the River of the Traders, as the seventeenth-century Indians who had bartered tobacco and catfish near my house called it. One Sunday my family took a hike on the towpath of the Chesapeake & Ohio Canal near Great Falls, 10 miles above Washington, D.C. where the broad river squeezes through an obstacle course of massive boulders and in just a half mile roars downward some 75 feet. Juno, our golden retriever, saw a squirrel and made a beeline down a tight path through a welter of vegetation. I followed and found myself on the edge of a 200-foot-high cliff overlooking the Potomac as she swirled through Mather Gorge, a granite defile that was described at the turn of the century as the Grand Canyon of the East. The sight was dazzling, the fast currents spinning the reflected light as though thousands of silver pinwheels were washing downstream. I was hypnotized, drawn toward the shimmering water, and I knew I had to get on that river.

Monday morning I announced to Miss Hammond, my English teacher, that I wanted to build a raft and journey down the Potomac just like Huckleberry Finn. She said fine, as long as I didn't miss any school. The long Memorial Day weekend was coming up, so I thought that would be the chance. I recruited my camping friends John Yost, Ricky Vierbuchen, Dave Nurney, Fred Higgins, and Steve Hatleberg, and we started gathering the equipment we'd need to build our raft and float the Potomac. We picked out an eight-mile run through Mather Gorge, one that expert kayakers had been running for years. Though, as we talked to the experts, including a scuba rescue team that routinely retrieved drowned bodies from the river, the prognosis was that we wouldn't make it through on a log raft; the rapids were too treacherous.

Word of our expedition spread through the student body, and the editor of the school newspaper, Dan Reifsnyder, approached me for the exclusive story. At 17 Dan was already hard-boiled, and he smelled disaster in my little plan. He made no pretense of looking for blood or a spectacular failure to fill column space in an upcoming issue. I said I was happy to give him the story, but I was certain he'd be disappointed: We planned to make it down the river on time and intact.

On Friday afternoon we set up camp not far below Great Falls and with axes and saws started cutting the timber we needed. We rolled the logs to our assembly spot down by the river and began binding them with cross pieces and eight-inch gutter nails. Our raft was about half-finished when a stentorian voice echoed across the canyon.

"Have you ever messed with a German shepherd?" It was a park ranger, calling from atop a palisade of gneiss on the Virginia side, a huge dog flanking him. "You're on national park land. You can't cut down trees, you can't build a raft, and you can't camp. Now get outta there before I come get ya."

It was the end of our dream trip. We slowly packed up and trudged back to the parking lot. On the drive out we passed a ranger vehicle coming in and guessed it was our friend with the German shepherd.

We still had two days of vacation left and couldn't go back home, not with everyone expecting us to have at least attempted our raft expedition. So, we headed for Bear Island, a popular camping spot below Mather Gorge, and holed up there for the rest of the long weekend, swimming, fishing, and trying to forget our failure.

Monday night we were back at my house cleaning the camping gear when the phone rang. It was Dan Reifsnyder and he wanted the scoop on our expedition. I put my hand over the receiver and talked to our team.

"Let's tell him we did it," I proposed with a grin.

"We can't," Steve Hatleberg countered. "It's not the Christian thing to do." In the *Adventures of Huckleberry Finn*, Huck had to battle with his conscience constantly. According to the morality of society and the church, he should have turned in Jim, the runaway slave; but Huck had come to love Jim like a brother. His final decision in Jim's favor was concluded with his famous reflection, "All right, then, I'll go to hell!"

I looked around at our group, then back at Steve, and said, "All right, then, I'll go to hell!" and I put the receiver to my mouth and started to tell Dan about our raft trip.

On June 9, the article appeared: "Rapids Capsize Craft; Raftsmen Score First." It went on to say, "The raft had to be scrapped in the middle of Yellow Rapids. 'We scrambled for the inner tubes and kept going,' boasted junior Richard Bangs . . . 'You wondered if you were going to live.' 'Man, was I scared.' 'It was out of sight, like an LSD trip.' These were just a few of the emotions described by the group, all of whom made the entire passage alive."

The article gave us some notoriety and inspired us to form The Raft Club, which would later become Sobek. (Named for the crocodile god of the river Nile, Sobek eventually became the world's premiere river-rafting organization.) Steve Hatleberg couldn't live with our secret though, and one day told Dan the true story. To Dan's credit, he never pursued it in print, but whenever I passed him in the hall he gave me that drop-dead stare that editors around the world have mastered. And, it made me want to make good on the Potomac.

It was still early summer when I saw an ad on the bulletin board at the grocery store: For sale, a 17-1/2-foot fiberglass Old Town canoe, $150. I called all the members of The Raft Club and asked if anyone would go in with me. Ricky Vierbuchen had the $75, so we bought the canoe, painted R&R on the stern (we flipped a coin for top billing), and toted our new toy down to Bear Island. We launched and headed upstream toward the crystalline mouth of Mather Gorge.

We were awkward paddlers, and the canoe crankled through the water as though drunk. We bobbed and weaved upstream, and slowly picked up some proficiency as we angled toward Difficult Run Rapids, marking the end of the gorge. The white-breasted water got faster as we got closer, and my blood flow accelerated as well. This was exciting. Then we were in the rooster tails of the rapid, being flung up and down on a dizzy aquatic seesaw, paddling with all our strength.

"Let's go higher," I screamed over the rapid's roar, and we sunk our blades deeper and lunged forward. The bow snapped to its side, abruptly capsizing the canoe, and throwing us into the spume. We'd been christened as river runners.

Ricky and I spent all our free time that summer in our blue canoe, exploring new routes, refining techniques, scoring the bottom of our boat with a matrix of scratches and dents. We made many of the classic runs, including the coup de grace of the Potomac beginning at the base of Great Falls, where the Potomac drops spectacularly over the edge of the continental bedrock onto the sedimentary soil of the coastal plain. Above Great Falls the river stretches to a half mile in width; below it pinches into the 60-foot-wide Mather Gorge, where we negotiated S-Turn Rapids, Rocky Island Rapids, Wet Bottom Chute, past the ancient rocks that formed the exit gate to the canyon. We continued downstream on a wider, but no less magnificent river, through Yellow Rapids and Stubblefield Falls, underneath the Cabin John Bridge carrying the Capital Beltway (I-495), past the Carderock Picnic Area where climbers crawled like flies on impossible faces, down to Sycamore Island and the Brookmont Dam. Constructed in the 1950s for the city water supply with no thought for the safety of boaters, the deceptively innocuous weir is a death trap for upset paddlers, with a perpetual hydraulic that, like a black hole with stray light, sucks in boats and bodies, and never lets them go. A sign adjacent to the pumping station states that an average of seven people drown in this area each year. Its nickname is the Drowning Machine.

Below Brookmont is the most exciting mile of navigable whitewater along the Potomac's entire 287-mile course, culminating in the explosive Little Falls, in which the entire river funnels from parking-lot width to a grand prix raceway and then is spectacularly split in two by a sharp granite-slab island. Here Captain John Smith, in his search for the elusive Northwest Passage, was stopped in his upriver journey in 1608. Little Falls is the last whitewater, or the first, depending on which way you're traveling on the Potomac. Just below is Chain Bridge. A little farther on the river becomes tidewater, and the nation's capital begins to spread its concrete tentacles along the banks.

Ricky and I never canoed the Little Falls section; it was beyond our abilities. But that didn't mean we couldn't run it. With the money I'd saved working as a car hop at the local Kentucky Fried Chicken outlet, I bought a yellow Taiwanese four-person raft from Sunny's Surplus. We paddled out to Snake Island, across from the Brookmont pumping station, and slipped over the killer weir where we thought the one clear passage, down a fish ladder, was supposed to be. But we missed and were suddenly in the backwashing hydraulic, capsized, bouncing about in the aerated water along with beach balls, chunks of cooler Styrofoam, rubber sandals, branches, and other debris stuck in the eternal washing machine. I remembered reading that the only way to escape a strong recirculating hydraulic was to abandon your life jacket and dive beneath the surface, where the water makes its deep water exit. But I couldn't bring myself to remove my flotation, which was propping my mouth just above the terrible soapy froth. I shot a hurried glance at Ricky, who was already choking on the water splashing into his throat.

"Let's swim toward the island," I yelled above the weir's gargling. And though it was slow going, we dog-paddled perpendicularly to the current, along the hydraulic line, and back toward Snake Island. I towed our little yellow raft, and after several scary minutes we reached the edge of the island, where a chute emptied water in a straight shot downstream. We were out and into the next section, where the water accelerated as the river narrowed, and the waves grew thicker with each few strokes. Then the final pitch presented itself, with the river piling up onto the anvil-shaped island, spilling off either side into huge, complex rapids. We blasted straight down the middle, plowed into the saber-toothed island, spun backward, and then collapsed over the falls on the Virginia side (the worst side). The first drop catapulted Ricky into the air. When he fell back into the bilge, the floor of the raft peeled back like a sardine can, depositing him into the depths. I continued to paddle alone, my feet dragging in the current where the floor had been, my head spinning around looking for signs of Ricky. The roar of the rapid muffled as I strained to hear Ricky's cry. Hours later, or so it seemed, Ricky resurfaced 50 yards downstream, all smiles. Climbing back on board, we paddled to our take-out at Chain Bridge on the Virginia side, where my mother was waiting with the Oldsmobile and a prayer.

I discovered the lack of floor didn't make much difference in the tiny Taiwanese boat and continued to use it for runs down Little Falls the following weeks with the various members of The Raft Club, even Steve Hatleberg, who thought he saw God during one capsize. For us it was the ultimate thrill in a suburban existence conspicuously short of any.

I fell in love with the Potomac that summer and wanted to know everything about her, every dimple, every curve, where she came from, and where she was going. I began to study her serpentine mysteries in my free time. She trickles forth at an altitude of 3,140 feet just downhill from the crest of Backbone Mountain in a deep fold of the Allegheny Mountains in Maryland. She seeps from a spring beneath a chunk of rock, called the Fairfax Stone after the colonial landowner Lord Fairfax. The fledgling river soon becomes the Maryland–West Virginia border, loops back and forth around Appalachian ridges in the region of the Paw Paw bends, and then bursts through the Blue Ridge Mountains at Harpers Ferry, where she is joined by the Shenandoah. Here the plunging slopes and roiling rapids make "perhaps one of the most stupendous scenes in nature," Thomas Jefferson wrote, "worth a voyage across the Atlantic." Continuing her journey, the Potomac levels off, now alive with geese and eagles, oysters and shad. She eventually becomes a seven-mile-wide tidal giant, easing majestically into Chesapeake Bay, as she stretches between the Maryland and Virginia shores.

13

As summer faded to fall, the frequency of our trips decreased because of the cooler weather, school commitments, and a new diversion. Ricky and I were both taken by a tall blonde named Arlene Wergen. The air surged with the dull clacking of soft, young antlers in nervous ritual combat. Since he shared homeroom and some classes with her, Ricky had the advantage. He took Arlene caving, camping, and bought her an expensive friendship ring. But I had an ace up my sleeve—the river. I just had to wait for the right moment.

It came in mid-December. We were having an unseasonal heat wave, and the weather forecaster said the upcoming weekend would be warm enough for outdoor activities. I asked Arlene if she'd like to go canoeing.

I picked out a run I had always wanted to do, a stretch beginning in West Virginia on the Shenandoah, running to the confluence with the Potomac, and continuing below Harpers Ferry, where John Brown's body lies a moulderin' in the grave. The 10-mile run was supposed to be beautiful, with some challenging rapids and good camping, all important ingredients in what I perceived to be an important weekend.

Saturday morning was clear and crisp as we loaded the blue canoe and headed downriver through a nave-like arch of sycamores and silver maples. The river here had sawed away at the mountains as they rose up beneath it, imbedding itself 1,200 feet and more in the Blue Ridge. I was wearing my new letter sweater, which I had been awarded for the dubious honor of managing the soccer team. Still it was a badge and I wore it proudly, hoping it would impress Arlene. It was a beautiful day, brimming with a sense of adventure and romance, and I could tell Arlene shared the thrill of a live vessel beneath us sliding silently over the brawling water. An ad for Canadian Club had been running that fall showing a couple canoeing the rapids. The woman in the bow looked very much like Arlene and, though I bore no resemblance, I felt like the man in the stern.

As we eased our way down the river, the sun's rays reflected off the water and I started to get warm. I took off my sweater and bundled it in front of my knees. At lunch we pulled over beneath a spreading willow, and I prepared a sumptuous repast with Pouilly-Fuissé, Brie, and French bread. As we took our first bites, a pint-sized bark came from behind us. A puppy bounded into our picnic. She was a mongrel, but with the biggest brown eyes I'd ever seen and a wiggly, irresistible appeal for affection. For Arlene it was puppy love. She fed the little mutt all of her meal, then some of mine, and then asked if we could bring her along.

"But she must belong to somebody," I protested.

"Please go check," she implored.

I got up to make a search. Sure enough I could find no evidence of owners within a mile of our mooring and I came to the conclusion the puppy was, indeed, hopelessly lost.

So we perched the puppy on my letter sweater and continued downriver. As the day wore on, the sky began to cloud and the temperature dropped. The puppy was asleep, so I didn't bother to put on my sweater but just paddled harder to keep warm. By late afternoon we approached the riverwide ledge of Bull Falls, which the guidebook rated as difficult but doable, recommending a portage for less-than-expert boaters. Checking my watch I saw we were at least an hour behind schedule; the puppy incident had taken up precious time. The guidebook said the portage around Bull Falls took an hour, an hour we didn't have on a short midwinter day. If we portaged, we'd have to paddle the final miles after dark, a dangerous proposition in the cold of December. And, after a full summer of canoeing, I figured I was more than "less than expert" and could make the run.

So, we rammed ahead into Bull Falls. The entry was perfect, gliding between the boulders as though on a track, slipping down the drop as though by design. At the bottom I held the canoe paddle above my head and screamed, "We made it!" But I was a bit premature. The tail waves at the bottom of the rapid continued to wash over the bow of the canoe, and the boat filled with the turbid Shenendoah. By the time we reached the last wave, we were swamped, and the canoe sluggishly rolled over, dispatching us into the icy river. The current was swift and the cold punched my breath away. With one hand I hung onto the canoe; with the other I tried to paddle, all the while yelling for Arlene to swim to shore. I saw my letter sweater surface a few feet away. That sweater meant the world to me, so I started paddling toward it when I heard a feeble yelp. The puppy was spinning in an eddy in the opposite direction. I weighed my options. I could only retrieve one.

A few hundred yards downstream I managed to grapple the canoe to shore, the puppy still held above my head with my free hand. Arlene was there, shivering violently, yet she gave the puppy a hug that would've crushed a bear. Both Arlene and I had lost our paddles in the capsize, though I had one spare strapped to the center thwart. I emptied the canoe, turned it over, and tried to tell Arlene to get back in—but my speech was slurred; I could barely form the words. I was becoming hypothermic. So was Arlene. I knew we couldn't stop. We had nothing dry and it was getting dark. We'd die if we stayed.

I pressed Arlene into the bow of the canoe, and she crouched over the trembling puppy, while I pushed off. I dug that one paddle into the river with all my strength. The sun dipped behind the trees, and a chilling wind blew up the valley. Barely able to see the rocks, I propelled us into the last rapids, the mile-long Staircase. We scraped and bumped and banged every few seconds, but somehow we emerged in one piece at the Route 340 bridge below Harpers Ferry, where my car was parked.

My plans for a romantic camp-out were scrapped that night. Rather than a hero, I was a bungler who'd almost cost us our lives, and worse, the life of the puppy, who had won the contest for Arlene's heart and soon became her constant companion.

Still, I remained hung up on Arlene, as did Ricky. But it was unrequited love. As the schoolyear wound down Arlene started dating a Young Republican, a radical act in the Vietnam era. When Ricky and I independently asked her to the senior prom, she turned us both down for the right-wing radical.

We'd been left high and dry. Neither of us found alternative dates for the most socially significant event of a teenager's life. So we turned to one another and said, "Let's go run a river."

We picked the Smoke Hole Canyon section of the South Branch of the Potomac in West Virginia for two reasons: We'd never done it before, and it was as far away from the prom as we could get and still be on our favorite river. So, as the senior class was slipping into crinoline and tuxedos, we were fitting our kneepads and life jackets. And as carnations were being exchanged, we were trading strokes on the upper Potomac. Mockingbirds called from the woods cathedral through which we passed, hardly giving us solace. It was springtime, and the delicate pink blossoms of the laurel and the notched white flowers of the dogwood dappled the greening banks. We moved to music, not the Motown our peers were enjoying but the haunting whistle of the lordly cardinal. The river here was shallow, stinging cold from the spring runoff. Some miles below our launch we struck a moss-encrusted rock, jutting out into the current like some miniature Lorelei. It punched a hole the size of my fist in our fiberglass hull.

We didn't have the materials nor the time to properly repair the boat, so we stuffed the puncture with spare clothing and continued downstream. It was slow going. We'd paddle 10 minutes, then pull over to bail for 10. When we pulled over to camp around twilight and emptied the canoe, we discovered that our neoprene duffel bag wasn't waterproof and all our gear, sleeping bags, tents, and food were soaked. We dragged everything up a knoll of weathered limestone, erected the wet tent, and spread the rest of our effects out to dry in the waning minutes of daylight.

It was soon evident that our attempts to dry the gear by natural means would not work and that it was getting cold. We had several packs of matches, but they were all wet. We gathered wood, and with our knives trimmed paper-thin shavings that would light at the least spark. But we went through several packs of matches and couldn't get that spark. With nightfall the air became bitter, and we jumped up and down,

slapping our sides, to keep warm. Our classmates were doing the Jerk in the Whitman gym, and we felt like the dance as we flapped in the dark. But it wasn't working, and I knew we couldn't do the Freddy all night. We needed to build a fire. If we didn't, we could die and we both knew it.

Then Ricky got a bright idea. The flashlight still worked, so why not unscrew the lens covering the bulb and put the remaining matches inside the glass, against the filament bulb, where they could dry from the heat of the light? We had five matches left, and inside they went. The flashlight remained on for 20 minutes as we continued our jumping jacks; then it started to fade. We unscrewed the top, took out the matches, and tried to light the first one. In my haste I tore off the head of the match. The second actually lit, but before I could touch it to the kindling, a cold wind extinguished it. I cupped my hand around the third as I struck and it spat to life. As I touched it to the shavings, the fire took. In minutes we had a bonfire. We dried our clothes and sleeping bags and bathed in the warmth all night, continuing to feed the fire and occasionally looking down the hill at the Potomac meandering in curves that somehow looked like Arlene's.

That was a special night, one filled with danger and promise, with rites of passage, with friendship and warmth. The Potomac had dealt some blows since our first assignation, but she had given me some of the most exciting, exquisite moments of my existence. On that prom night, high on a limestone ridge, I realized I really loved that river and that I had found a consort for life. I discovered, as Tom Sawyer finally said to Huckleberry Finn, that all I really wanted to do was "have adventures plumb to the mouth of the river." On that prom night I lost and found a certain innocence and readied for the adventures of tomorrow, the great adventures cached just around the next bend.

15

Steven Michael Lowe

16

Although out-of-focus, this photo shows the first successful run in an open canoe of the last drop on the Virginia side of Great Falls of the Potomac River. The falls, 10 miles above Washington, D.C., drop 77 feet in three-quarters of a mile. The falls are created where the Potomac, like all other rivers that flow eastward into the Atlantic, drops over the edge of the continental bedrock onto the sedimentary soil of the coastal plain.

Steven Michael Lowe

Early morning sun illuminates the forest along Maine's Kennebec River.

KENNEBEC

The Gem of Maine

Skinny, 18, and decidedly agnostic about the sacrament awaiting me, I stepped onto the 33-foot-long bridge-pontoon raft to cast my fate to the river at Lees Ferry on a hot April day in 1969. This was the Colorado, the grandad of great rivers, and I was to be a "swamper," an all-around gofer, on the cook boat that would service the 110 members of the Four Corners Geological Society who had chartered this experience. This was my first trip west, my first commercial raft trip, my first job. And looking around at the tanned, thickset, cocksure boatmen, I felt out-of-sync, out-of-place. Then as we pushed off, and started introductions among our crew, I discovered a kindred spirit: fellow swamper Jim Ernst. He was my age; this, too, was his first Colorado trip; and he was from back East.

The trip was a turning point in my life, a watershed if you will, in that it propelled me toward a career with wild rivers. And though he took a different channel, it was the same for Jim Ernst. After several more trips as swampers, we both graduated to become full-fledged river guides for Hatch River Expeditions and spent the next several summers as river-gods in the bottom of the Grand Canyon. Then in the winter of 1973 I went off to run rivers in Africa and started my own company, Sobek, which I envisioned running rivers around the world in the off-season, allowing me to return in the summers to my first love. When Hatch heard of my moonlighting, he sent me a letter in Ethiopia politely terminating my employment, saying they had to cut back on staff because of the oil crisis.

The letter saddened me. It meant I would no longer be working with my friends in a place I truly loved. That summer I did manage to find some free-lance work on the Colorado with other companies, but it wasn't the same. Occasionally I passed Jim Ernst guiding a Hatch boat and we exchanged waves. He looked happy, secure in his pilot's seat. I wondered if my ambition had botched a good thing. And I was jealous of Jim.

I no longer had steady employment on the Colorado, so I dedicated more time to developing Sobek. But through the rumor mill, I continued to hear about the doings of my former colleagues. In 1976 a piece of gossip filtered into my apartment that gave me pause. Jim Ernst, after running 101 trips down the Colorado through the Grand Canyon for Hatch River Expeditions, had up and quit. He had moved back to Maine and had formed his own company that would be offering trips down a newly discovered rafting run. What was the name of this river that could entice Jim from the greatest river in America, from one of the best jobs on the planet? My source said it was called the Kennebec. It sounded magical.

In the mid-1970s rafting was quickly moving from rebel sport to mainstream recreation. Some rivers were becoming too crowded; guides called it people pollution. Others were being dammed. And a few new stretches were being discovered. The Kennebec was one of the discoveries of this era. For over a decade when the inevitable campfire debates over America's top 10 wild rivers took place, the Kennebec cropped up, and I thought of Jim Ernst and became envious. Finally, after more than a dozen years without contact, I wrote Jim a letter, saying I wanted to make a Labor Day journey across country to come and float his famous river. I never heard back from Jim, but instead got a call from his friendly neighborhood rival, Wayne Hockmeyer, who said, "Come on out. Let me show you what we got."

For seven years Wayne Hockmeyer was a waterbed entrepreneur in the Boston area, and although he made money, he hated city life. A Tufts University dropout, he had done some sky diving and skin diving, had been a bush pilot in Canada, had hunted big game in Uganda, and, to certify his eccentricity, had piloted a canoe down Maine's snow-covered Squaw Mountain. Those moments had given him a keen sense of the fullness of life, had sent his pulse soaring. Waterbeds didn't do that. So, he chucked it all and moved north to west-central Maine's Moosehead Lake to become a hunting and fishing guide.

On the eastern outlet of Moosehead, a sparkling stream bounds to life beneath a dam. The Abnaki Indians, who combed its banks for flint, named it *Kennebec* meaning "serpent." It sprints for 3 spirited miles, then purls into an artificial rest stop, the 9-mile-long Indian Pond, created in 1954 by the 155-foot-high Harris Station hydroelectric dam, named for a former chief engineer of Central Maine Power Company. Below the dam

the East Branch of the Kennebec roars into high gear, and spits into a 12-mile-long steep granite gorge, before slipping into neutral at the confluence with the Dead River. It continues on a jagged southeastern course for another 150 miles until it empties, unceremoniously, into the Atlantic just below Bath.

In the spring of 1976 Wayne was thrashing around the woods looking for a good fishing hole, when he parted the branches on a beetling ledge and looked down into a deep, swirling pool, isolated and ideal for landlocked salmon and trout. The only problem was this little back eddy on the Kennebec was too isolated, too inaccessible for most of his clients. They would have to be lowered in by ropes. He gazed upriver, then down, and saw a fast-moving, relatively smooth, wild river. Why not boat clients down to this spot?

Before committing to such a scheme, Wayne sent river-flow data and topographic maps to Jon Dragon who ran a successful rafting operation down the New River in West Virginia. Dragon told Wayne to forget it—the gradient was too steep and he'd probably die if he tried it. But that didn't stop Wayne. He was broke and he needed a new angle to bring in the anglers. He hired a plane and flew over the river. He didn't really know what to look for, but from the air it didn't look that bad.

His admonitions notwithstanding, Dragon sold Wayne a used 22-foot-long British Leyland cotton neoprene raft, which Wayne dubbed the *Silver Bullet*. He snookered eight bear hunters from New Jersey into joining him for a free run down the Kennebec from its source, neglecting to tell his passengers it was a first descent. It was May, and the water was cold and high from the spring freshet. No one on the run had ever been rafting before.

Wayne had seen the movie *River of No Return*, in which Robert Mitchum steers Marilyn Monroe down the Salmon with a sweep oar in the back of his log raft, and so he figured that was the way to do it. He positioned himself in the back with a canoe paddle as tiller and shoved off in a driving rainstorm. Despite the inclement weather, the trip down the first three miles was lively and fun, through some sizable rapids, down some major chutes. The paddle across Indian Pond was uneventful but scenic. They portaged around Harris Station dam, launched again, and the fireworks began.

Almost immediately they were out of control, flailing paddles, hanging on for their lives as they flew over waves, pitched into dark holes, and were repeatedly deluged. The Kennebec was a logging river, the last in the United States, and as the raft rolled over the haystacks, cut timber pitched past, sometimes missing them by inches. Finally after half a dozen miles, they managed to wrestle the swamped boat to shore, where one of the hunters fell to his knees and kissed the muddy ground.

They had neglected to bring any bailing buckets, so they used baseball caps instead. They had no wet suits, so they shivered onshore as they reviewed their ordeal.

When Wayne said "Let's get back in and get going," the bear hunters took pause and discussed hiking out. To some this whole endeavor was too crazy, too macho. But Wayne's enthusiasm won them over and back they went for more whitewater pummeling. When the raft got turned around, they decided to all turn around as well and continue paddling facing forward. None had heard of backpaddling.

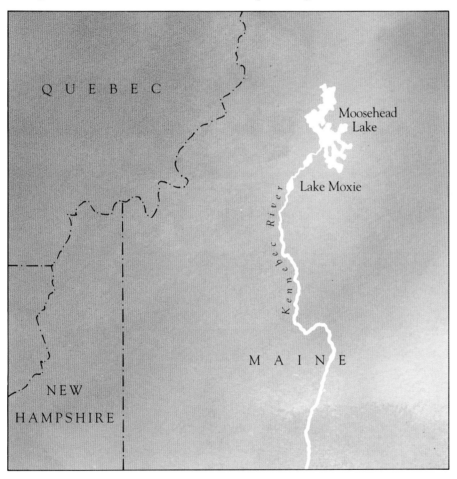

They didn't do much fishing on that maiden voyage. Most were grateful to have survived. Wayne, however, had been baptized, and northeastern river running was about to undergo a dramatic parthenogenesis. This was great sport, the most exhilarating thing Wayne had ever done. Scrap the fishing guide stuff, he thought, I'm going to be a river guide and take people down this river for fun and profit.

Wayne's timing couldn't have been better. For more than a century the Kennebec had been a chief thoroughfare for moving logs down to Augusta, where the river becomes tidal. From the early 1800s to the 1920s the preferred wood was pine, which was stripped and hewed for masts. With the advent of steel boats, timber barons shifted their cutting and their log drives to the fir and spruce (which produce the best pulp) used in the paper mills on the middle Kennebec. When log runs were happening, the river was choked with dangerous timber that would pose enormous threats to boaters. Yet, in 1976 environmentalists convinced the Maine legislature to pass a law prohibiting log runs down the Kennebec. The reasons had nothing to do with rafting: The rotting bark from the floating logs sank to the bottom of the river and depleted the oxygen in the water, killing the fish. Now, for the first time in over a century, the river would run clear.

Wayne hung up his rods, printed some brochures, and opened up an instant classic. In his first year of operation, he herded 600 clients to the Kennebec in a second-hand cattle truck, sent them rolling down the river, and lost $8,000. Worse, he attracted competition.

Less than a year after the maiden voyage, Jim Ernst heard about Wayne's new run and decided to jump in headfirst as well. He created Maine Whitewater, Inc., and brought what he had learned on the Colorado to the Northeast—proper rafting equipment and techniques. Word spread and within a couple of years thousands were taking raft trips down the Kennebec with over a dozen different outfitters. In 1988 over 30,000 people took the plunge, about one-fifth with Wayne Hockmeyer's company, Northern Outdoors.

Where the Dead River meets the Kennebec is a pause in the stream-of-consciousness drive up Route 201 called the Forks. There Wayne and Suzie Hockmeyer built their pine-log Kennebec Base Lodge (this was the second incarnation; the first burned New Year's Eve 1983) to serve their river clients, more than 75,000 by the end of 1988.

The start of Labor Day weekend I arrived at Wayne and Suzie's 100-acre spread (a resort complete with paddle tennis court, hot tub, sauna, logominiums, and a stone fireplace facing a long bar, for après-rafting), and sat down to a meal called The Rafter (ham and Swiss floating in mayonnaise) and a dessert called Death by Chocolate.

Wayne and Suzie told me of the ups and downs of their rafting business, of the political storms they'd weathered to keep their concern going, and of the adventures they'd shared on the rivers, including the nearby Penobscot, another popular run pioneered by Wayne.

A man of sometimes shrill polemics, Wayne had lived Churchill's prediction that those with hearts and heads would be liberal at adolescence and conservative at middle age. Wayne had just turned 50 and, while in his early rafting years he had been instrumental in defeating the proposed Cold Stream Dam on his section of the river, he is now an outspoken supporter of the upstream Harris Station dam, which supplies the constant flows that make his rafting concern viable. To the chagrin of

21

many environmentalists, the man who had formed the "Protect the Kennebec and Penobscot Society" in the 1970s had in the 1980s made deals with the Great Northern Paper Company and Central Maine Power Company who control dams on the Penobscot and Kennebec, respectively, to pay them a percentage of his client take to keep his rivers running. Wayne has repeatedly butted heads with the purist preservationists, who claim he has turned a wilderness area into a commercial water slide.

Regardless of his politics, in just 12 years Wayne had emerged as the godfather of northeastern rafting, the man who had saved the river from the disparate yet equally ignoble fates of too much environmental protection (and thus no access to recreational boaters) and too much commercial exploitation (dams and water-releasing policies suiting only electrical power needs, thus not providing reliable and sufficient flows to conduct scheduled rafting trips).

Suzie Hockmeyer (née Yeaton of Andover), 37, Wayne's honeylocked, diminutive wife of 17 years, a gifted athlete and consummate outdoorsperson, is known as the Queen of the Kennebec, the first woman licensed as a whitewater guide in Maine, who now has logged over 400 descents, the world record. While Wayne admitted to being a bit battle weary in his backwoods retreat, Suzie's eyes still sparkled, especially when talking of her turf, the river experience, rather than the backroom politics that suck down so many heros, like rubber duckies in a whirlpool. Together they made a team whose power doubled the sum of its parts and kept the Kennebec adventure alive and available, efficient yet romantic. We swapped river stories and clinked glasses deep into the evening, three old salts drowning in good memories of haystacks and hydraulics past.

The next morning a loon let me know it was time to find the wet suit and get going. We were near where the sun's rays first hit the United States on clear days, and splinters of light through a cloud cover were trying to demonstrate that distinction. Out in front of the lodge, Suzie handed out factory-identical paddles to her clients. "You want a left-handed or a right-handed paddle?" she asked in seemingly earnest tones, and Pam, a photographer in our group, asked for a right-handed one before she realized the joke.

We filed onto an old school bus, as though kindergartners on the first day of school. As with most river trips, we were a mixed grill about to share the fire. Somewhat awkwardly we exchanged bits of information about ourselves. My rafting partners included Melanie, a travel agent from Boston; Larry of Rhode Island real estate; Karen, a French teacher also from Rhode Island; and Bob, a Massachusetts appliance store owner. Shelby, a 21-year-old powerlifter and 9-year whitewater veteran, would row Pam, the photographer, in a separate Avon raft. I was the only one who flew from California for the weekend to make this one-day raft trip.

With the huge steering wheel in Suzie's 110-pound command, we trundled 40 minutes upstream over an ancient train bed to the Harris Station dam, a hive of activity where boats were being pumped up, life jackets fitted, and frames carted. It reminded me of my first arrival at Lees Ferry almost 20 years earlier, only now I was no longer skinny, a schoolboy, or an agnostic in the church of wild rivers, and the guides were more of a demographic sampling: women, teenagers, Yuppies, and graybeards. But the same sense of anticipation charged the air, like the moments before an electrical storm. The clients nervously paced the platform above the dam and stared down into 4,800 cubic feet per second of troubled water issuing from the dam's three turbines, water that would bear them downstream into unknown thrills and dangers. An edict from Central Maine Power was posted at the railing: *Warning: Before launching any craft, please read. For the next few miles, this river can be extremely dangerous and you may be injured or lose your life.* It was enough to give an old rafter pause.

I felt a quickening of my pulse and a dryness in my throat as we pushed the banana-yellow Domar into the eddy and climbed on board. Queen Suzie would be our paddle captain, barking commands at the stern of the boat, while Wayne would accompany us in his 10-foot, red polyethylene Aquanautic kayak.

As we bobbed in the eddy at 800 feet above sea level, waiting our turn among the score of other rafts and fighting off the Maine state birds, the black flies that feasted on our anticipatory sweat, I looked back at Suzie in the rear, arms cocked and ready and I couldn't help but admire the Slavic lines of her face and her earth-toned skin. Suzie was a woman at peace with the river, with the wilderness, with herself. Then, with a scream, she broke my reverie: "Let's hit it!"

We pointed downstream and, like desperate treasure hunters, dug our paddles into the foam. Almost immediately we were cast into class IV rapids, the Three Sisters. We plunged down the middle, riding a vector into two of the sisters, flirting with the skirt of the third. The banks were a peripheral blur as we nipped the edge of the Goodbye Hole. With barely a breather for bailing with our plastic buckets, we were into the Alleyway, a narrow corridor packed with standing waves that alternately sent us flying skyward and buried us in avalanches of water. Uncorked tempests seemed to assail us from all sides. It was dreamlike, sailing through a delirium of wanton crests and troughs.

After two miles of rhapsodic whitewater, we pulled into an eddy to bail, now fully initiated, and looked up for the first time. We were in The Cathedral, a quiet chamber that elicits reverence for its natural beauty. The canyon that cradled us was geologically an infant, formed 10,000 years ago when water froze between rocks and then thawed, cracking the gorge like an egg. The granite walls looked as if they'd been sculpted by a master, rimmed with arrow-straight pines and their twisted sisters, the red cedars. Between bails, I looked around. Everyone was grinning, even Wayne, who indoors tends toward the dour. This experience was his creation, and it was one that had speed-pumped the blood of thousands, made them laugh, put them in awe of nature's best work, and instilled, if just for a day, a feeling that life really is exciting.

But there was little time for pondering. This was Sunday and, despite Wayne's negotiations with the powers that be, the river would be turned off at 2:00. We had to get through Magic Falls before then, or the rafting would be over and we'd have to hike out.

Magic is the monster that everyone fears and fantasizes about. Most of the spectacular photos of people being catapulted like champagne corks, of rafts capsizing that adorn the walls of the Kennebec Base Lodge, are of Magic.

Wayne named the nine-foot falls 12 years ago during his first commercial rafting season, because his rafts would disappear into its maw, then magically reappear downstream, not infrequently upside down. Daily throughout the summer, photographers and rubberneckers would make the two-mile trek down a snowmobile trail to a vantage just above Magic where they could witness, as if in the Colosseum, participants being thrown to the lions.

Now we were approaching Magic, and the tension was so thick it could have been cut with a paddle. I tried whistling "Do You Believe in Magic?" but stopped when the others gave me dirty looks. Suzie told us that the falls were too big to keep paddling through. At her command, a second before impact, everyone had to stop paddling and grab a safety rope to stay in.

Then, too soon, we were in it. My peripheral vision caught a small crowd on the shore, hoping for a spectacle—a capsize or worse. We slid down the tongue toward a bellowing backboil that snapped at us with white fangs, and Suzie screamed, "Hold on now!" There was no hesitation. I shouldered over the bow, a lineman going for a tackle, hoping to keep the bow down so it wouldn't capsize end-over-end. And the mountain collapsed . . . tons of water seemed to pound my back, my sides, my face. The universe was a tearing, terrifying rush of gray-white—and we were through it. I opened my eyes and couldn't see. We must've capsized, I thought, we must be underwater.

But I heard voices, cascades of laughter. I blinked and blearily saw we were upright, but realized my glasses, which had been secured around my head by a tight rubber string called a croakie, were gone. I swirled my hands in the bilge, which was brimming with water, and found the glasses floating near my knees. Putting them on, I joined the giddiness of our survival. We'd submarined through Magic, plowed through the middle of the wave, and emerged the right way on the other side, everything dampened but our enthusiasm. What had been a nervous little ship of fools just moments before was now a destroyer full of soldiers triumphantly sailing out of the Straits of Hormuz. It was cause for joy.

Guiltily grinning through his Vandyke, Wayne paddled up next to us and pointed to his kayak, suffering from a dent that scored half the boat. Wayne had dropped into Magic just behind us but didn't emerge quite as felicitously. The hole held onto Wayne and spun him around, battering his boat and letting him know that, despite his revered status as the King of the Kennebec, the river ruled, now as always.

The rest of us were heady with our victory, so we fearlessly paddled through Carry Brook rapids and to the eddy of the same name where we pulled in for lunch. The area was named by the early explorers who portaged their birchbark canoes around the upstream rapids and returned their boats to the river at a little brook just upstream, thus "Carry Brook." Benedict Arnold followed this route with 1,100 men on his aborted invasion of Canada in the fall of 1775.

Having made a few one- and two-day raft trips throughout the West, I figured lunch here would be the standard fare: sandwiches, cookies, Kool-Aid, maybe a fruit or guacamole salad to add some panache. I never expected haute cuisine: steaks and fresh fish cooked over a bonfire, stir-fry in a giant wok, "Maine Guide Coffee" (two raw eggs with shells dropped into the pot with water and coffee and boiled three times), freshly baked cookies, trail mix, and iced lemonade made from sweet, untreated Kennebec water. It was enough to bring tears to a cataracted eye. I'd never seen a hot lunch on a river trip, but I'd never been to Maine, where the weather can change into four seasons in as many minutes—and it did. The sunny skies that looked over Magic just minutes before were nowhere to be found; dark clouds, looking like bruises, rolled over our little wilderness depot, and spat down a cold drizzle, which made the steak taste like warm manna from heaven. It was easy to see how someone who loves whitewater and good food could become a "Maineiac."

Lunch was too good, and we lingered too long. By the time we were ready to relaunch to finish the run, the river had already started to drop. The dam had been shut, and the river would soon be reduced to a trickle. We hustled into the raft and started paddling downstream on a river with half its morning muscle. We bounced through Black Brook rapids, usually a class III, but now barely on the scale. We passed osprey nests crowning tall king pines, broods (or is it gaggles?) of merganser ducks all in a row, and the Moxie tributary, which hosts a 90-foot falls named after

23

the Hockmeyer's springer spaniel (or maybe it's the other way around). The last rapids, Stand-Up Rips, were almost worth their name, as we repeatedly hung up on shallow rocks and had to get out and push. Then, after six of the most satisfying hours to be had anywhere in the Northeast, we pulled into a landing near the Route 201 bridge, on the road to Quebec.

In an hour we were back at the lodge sipping hot toddies and reviewing the photos and video taken of our run through Magic. Everyone, of course, was thrilled to relive the dramatic moments of high adventure as seen from the shore perspective, but after the third showing I grew a bit weary and my mind wandered. I turned to Suzie and asked if she knew my old rafting associate, Jim Ernst.

"Oh sure, he just lives down the road. He used to be our enemy, back when we were fierce competitors. But, that's all patched up and we're good friends now. In fact, he called us after he got your letter. Want me to see if he's home?"

Tentatively, I shook my head. I was a little concerned since he hadn't answered my note. Perhaps he didn't want to see me. "Ask if you can bring a surprise guest to dinner," I suggested.

Two hours later we pulled into the Gadabout Gaddis airport on the banks of the Kennebec on the outskirts of Bingham. Jim now owned this small airstrip, as well as a restaurant and his rafting concern. We knocked on the door and Eliza and Jim Ernst answered. Jim recognized me immediately and I him. He barely looked older than when I had last seen him on the Colorado 15 years before. We exchanged the usual pleasantries, and then he softly described his quiet life on the Kennebec. Though we

were the same age with similar formative experiences, he seemed different from me now. He seemed to have arrived at an armistice with the battles of life, on the edge of the wilderness, next to a wild river.

We walked the short distance to his restaurant and stepped inside. Its most distinguishing feature was a hot tub overlooking the dining area. At a table looking out over the Kennebec, we sat down to share a bottle of California Zinfandel, but before it appeared, Jim excused himself, disappeared out the door and reappeared a moment later leading a llama. Llama raising was his latest passion; he hoped to breed them. Once again, he was experimenting with a lifestyle business on the fringe and, looking into the animal's soft, liquid, plum-sized eyes, I couldn't help but feel a pang of envy.

"Why didn't you answer my note?" I asked over dinner.

"I'm sorry," he said. "But I never got around to it. Things are slower here. And I like that. I have no desire to run the Zambezi or even travel overseas. I like it here. When winter comes I close up shop, watch the snow fall on the river, and curl up on the couch with a good read."

We toasted a few more times and then exchanged a good-bye hug, promising we wouldn't wait so long to catch up on one another next time, a pledge that rang false. As Wayne and Suzie drove me back up Route 201 paralleling the Kennebec, I couldn't help but wonder who took the correct path when we each left the Colorado so many miles ago. I had elected quantity and complexity, chalking up rivers around the world. Jim had chosen the simplicity and quality of a single, very special river. His was the road not taken, and I had miles to go before I could sleep easy, knowing now the river where Jim's journey had led.

Wayne Hockmeyer running the river he made popular—Maine's Kennebec.

Lynn Stone

Richard Bangs rafting the 12-mile-long run of the East Branch of the Kennebec with Northern Outdoors, the pioneering company owned by Wayne and Suzie Hockmeyer. The river issues from Moosehead Lake and continues on a jagged southeastern course for 150 miles until it empties into the Atlantic just below Bath, Maine.

28

Pamela Roberson

Suzie Hockmeyer, Queen of the Kennebec with over 400 descents, piloting her raft into the witchcraft of Magic Falls. Wayne Hockmeyer named these falls Magic in 1976 during his first commercial rafting season because his rafts would disappear into the maw, then magically reappear downstream, not infrequently upside-down.

Pamela Roberson

Long Creek, South Carolina, a Chattooga River tributary.

CHATTOOGA

A Matter of Deliverance

It was the end of the summer of 1972. It had been a season of deliriously good times on the Colorado and, as was the common practice among river guides, I pulled out my address book of passengers—all those customers who had survived the rapids with me at the helm and who at trip's end had implored with teary conviction that I must come visit whenever the opportunity presented itself. Los Angeles seemed a proper juxtaposition, a nice place to spend a couple of weeks after four months in the wilderness. So, with fellow river rats John Yost, Lewis Greenwald, and Rick Szabo I took off for the bright lights and the big city.

We stayed with a family in San Marino, fashionably northeast of L.A., and explored the sites, the beach, restaurants, museums. And we quickly got bored. Then we noticed an event that promised to elevate the urban experience—the opening of the film *Deliverance*.

James Dickey's tour de force of violent adventure and inner discovery on a fictitious southeastern river had become an instant classic with its publishing in 1970, and for river runners it was the Talmud. Now, John Boorman had brought the tale to the big screen, and the world premiere was at the Cinerama Dome in Hollywood.

The entrance to the theater was decked out with ravaged river gear, splintered paddles, and ripped life jackets. From the ceiling hung an aluminum Grumman, severely bashed and dented. The tenor was right and, as we surrendered to the darkness of the theater, the story was so real, so frightening, so powerful that the images were singed on my mind. I identified with Ed, played by Jon Voight, the WASPish city boy-man, who was one of life's sliders until he found a concealed inner strength through his confrontation with the river. I saw my friend Lewis as the Lewis of the film, who plows into the experience with abandon, believing he is immortal, and is near fatally injured in the process.

When we emerged into the street, we turned to one another and almost simultaneously asked the same question: "Where was that river?"

It was the Chattooga, we later learned, running between Georgia and South Carolina. And we all vowed to run it someday.

Three years later my good friend and original partner in Sobek, Lewis Greenwald, was drowned on the Blue Nile in Ethiopia when his raft capsized and his life jacket caught in the stern line. Like the Lewis in *Deliverance*, he had gone too far, only this wasn't fiction. Lewis paid for his gung-ho spirit with his life. I wasn't on the trip. I'd taken some time away from rivers to pursue graduate studies. John Yost called to give me the news. It sent me into a tailspin.

What sort of Faustian bargain had I struck, I wondered. I had spent 10 years challenging wild rivers around the country and in East Africa and had amassed more than my fair share of thrills and spills. Now, my close friend was dead. Suddenly the thought of rafting down a river seemed evil, a frivolous exercise that had such an insidious downside that I couldn't imagine why people would risk it. The thought of laughing while paddling through the raised fist of a wave, a slap of whitewater that could knock a person unconscious and suck the life from a precious body, was abhorrent, pornographic, insane. I wanted to call all my past passengers and tell them the truth about river running and urge them to stay away from rafts and rivers.

My attitude about rivers had bent like a Canyonlands gooseneck. Rivers didn't assert life; they took it away. They weren't innocent; they were dissolute. I didn't ever want to go near a wild river again. I hung up my paddle.

I buried myself in studies that winter and tried to forget the pain I associated with river running and with the loss of Lewis. But, as the months wore on I began to soften. Friends would stop by my apartment on their way to run a river, and when I tried to explain my hostility for what they were doing, their eyes glassed over. And, at social functions, I couldn't ignore the palpable excitement across the room when talk finally did steer to rivers run and yet to be. That spring my most exciting endeavor was watching the tomatoes grow.

Early summer I headed east with John Yost for a visit with our families. Rick Szabo was also on the Atlantic seaboard finishing graduate school. When the three of us got together for a reunion, John suggested we pick up on our vow of a few years back and run the Chattooga. Rick loved the idea; I hated it. I had sworn off rivers, and wanted nothing to do with it—especially the Chattooga, which evoked thoughts of death and memories of Lewis. Resistance rose in me like marble.

But John and Rick persisted, saying it would be fun and perhaps therapeutic. It was supposed to be an especially beautiful river, and the rapids, though challenging, were not unduly dangerous. In fact, in the wake of *Deliverance,* the river had become one of the most popular in the country, with some 50,000 boaters running its rapids each year, up from the 800 who had floated it in 1971, the year before the film was released, and the 100 who had run the river in 1967. In the end, as with all my resolutions, I capitulated. It did sound like fun and I had been in a bad mood for months.

With another high school friend, Steve Jovanovich, we piled into my mother's Oldsmobile and headed south to run the *Deliverance* river. We got out of the car at Bryson City, North Carolina, home of the Nantahala Outdoor Center, the southeastern river runners' mecca. The air was so thick with humidity, you could pick it up and throw it. It was a major relief just to step inside the log cabin shop. There we met owner Payson Kennedy, who had been the stunt double for Burt Reynolds on some of the hairier canoeing scenes in the movie. Over some salt pork and sowbelly, Payson told us about something he called the *Deliverance* Syndrome, a phenomenon that the film and book incited. Despite its message of ill-conceived adventures and death, thousands of viewers had been inspired to come and boat the Chattooga. Many had had no whitewater experience and were improperly outfitted when they headed downriver. There had been too many drownings in the past few years attributed to boating under the *Deliverance* influence, and Payson saw no end in sight. Then he invited us to share a few beers before we headed down to the river. We drank and laughed as he told stories of the fools who headed down the river without life jackets or spare paddles and never came back. Laughing on the outside, crying on the inside, I again began to doubt my decision.

The next morning we headed for our encounter with the Chattooga. The river begins its life as a clear trickle near Cashiers, North Carolina, adjacent to Whiteside Mountain. It hooks and cramps for 50 miles through the blue-hazed Appalachians, dropping a vertical half mile in the process, until it succumbs to the static waters of Lake Tugaloo.

Through the years, few people had enjoyed the river's beauty. The Cherokees had a large settlement on its banks prior to 1700 and they gave the river its name, *Chattooga,* meaning "place of the white rocks." The first white settlers did not come to the river until the 1800s, and because the land was so rugged, there were not many of them. Loggers worked the river in the early part of this century. Towns grew nearby in later years, but still the Chattooga stayed wild. The local people fished for trout and redeye bass, camped, and swam in the cold water.

But as the 1960s grew to a close, something new arrived. Young outlanders, usually from the city, began showing up with canoes, kayaks, and rafts strapped to their cars. At first, they trickled in, but each year their numbers grew. The locals didn't quite know what to make of them. And then, to further complicate matters, *Deliverance* came along.

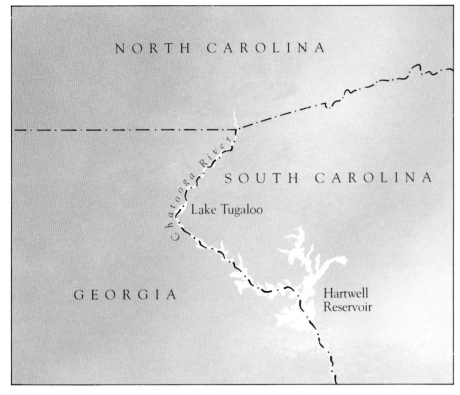

For most of its course, the Chattooga divides South Carolina and Georgia, creating the boundary between the Sumter and Chattahoochee national forests. The Chattooga remains one of the last free-flowing streams in the Southeast. In 1974 it qualified for federal protection under Wild and Scenic status. (In 1968 the U.S. government created a Wild and Scenic Rivers System to provide federal protection for rivers in much the same way that parklands are protected. Certain criteria—scenic, recreational, geologic, historic, and cultural value as well as fish and wildlife populations—are evaluated in selecting the rivers. Once chosen, the rivers are protected from dams, diversion projects, and riverside development that would alter their character.)

The Chattooga is divided into four sections, each more difficult than the one before. We set our sights on section IV, dropping 30 feet per mile. But, to get into the spirit of the river, we decided to run the last rapid on section III first. We carried our raft 300 yards upstream to a rapid

called Bull Sluice, one that the guidebook recommended portaging.

The river valley sloped gently, covered with white pine and hemlock, dogwood and sourwood, rhododendron and laurel. Beyond, a mountain loomed, high, broad, and blue, the color of concentrated wood smoke. I looked out over the white caps of the rapid and expected to see bursting knives lashing at the sky; but instead the rapid looked inviting, more like cream on cappuccino.

I took my position in the raft, the right stern, where I would act as paddle captain, and we pushed off into the river. The current entered my muscles and body as though I were carrying it; it came up through the paddle. We dropped 10 feet in two successive waterfalls and practically shot through the hydraulic at the bottom. It was a rousing ride, one that had us all whooping at its conclusion. I looked skyward and quoted from the film, the words that Bobby (Ned Beatty) spoke after running their first major section of rapids: "I tell you Lewis, that's the best—the second best sensation I ever felt." I was coming back, and it felt good.

We paddled under the silver bridge and were immediately surfing through more rapids. There was no sensation of the water's raging, but rather of its alertness and resourcefulness as it split apart at rocks, frothed lightly, corkscrewed, fluted, fell, recovered, jostled over smoothed stones, and then ran out of sight along garden-staircase steps around another turn. Usually soft-spoken, I was screaming as we worked to the right and blasted through Screaming Left Turn. We hopped from eddy to eddy into a jumble of rocks, where I called out a bad command, and we paddled smack into a boulder, which spun us around and sent us falling backward into a series of holes. Then we tumbled into a quiet cove, where we pulled in our paddles and I bent to catch my breath. The thrill of running rapids had come back, but I was out of practice, out of shape. And the most dangerous rapid was next.

We pulled over to scout Woodall Shoals, rated VI, which the guidebook said was suitable only for a "crazed team of experts." All others were supposed to portage. A granite ledge jutted from the left bank, forcing the current into a narrow channel. The river dropped over the ledge with a roar, sending up a perpetual spindrift. I stared into the infamous hole at the bottom of these falls. It didn't look that bad, though a tightly coiled, powerful wave was recirculating at its lower end. This was the killer hole that had, since the movie's release, refused to release so many bodies. But as I scrutinized the water dynamics, I knew we could get through it if we just kept the raft dead-on straight.

I was repulsed and drawn at the same time, desperately frightened, but also calm. A part of me, a cerebral side, told me that portaging was the judicious thing to do. Otherwise we would be attempting high-risk water, the type of water that had killed Lewis. But another side, an emo-

33

tional, irrational, adrenaline-fueled side, wanted to run Woodall Shoals. I felt we could do it and I wanted to do it.

"Let's run it," I said.

Yost and Rick were psyched. Steve, who was new to the sport, wasn't so sure. But he climbed in and assumed his position in the bow.

As we approached the tongue, I pointed the raft like an arrow directly downstream and instructed that nobody paddle until I gave the command. I had to keep the boat straight, and I would do it by letting the current propel our craft while I ruddered in the back. Just before we dropped into the hole, Steve inexplicably shot his paddle into the current for a quick stroke. I watched in horror as the water broke around his blade like glass, and the boat turned slightly. I couldn't correct it, and we washed into the hole at an angle, just what we didn't want. The raft bucked and kicked and rose to ride over the hydraulic, then it stalled. I drove the paddle deep. If the raft slipped back, we would be caught in the death trap. We hung at the rounded crest of the hydraulic for an eternity—the raft and the wave like two wrestlers locked in a trembling stalemate, waiting for one to give. The fabric beneath us seemed to shudder as though it were about to explode, and then suddenly we shot to the other side, safe and sound. We erupted in self-congratulatory cheers.

Below Woodall Shoals we passed a Forest Service road, and then the banks grew steeper and the river began to narrow to less than half its upstream width. The canyon walls were gray, limestonish, pitted, and scabby. We were committed now. There was no way out except downstream. We bounced through Double Dip, careened over Seven Foot Falls, and had a close encounter with Alligator Rock, which took a snap at us, grazed the side of the raft, but left no scars.

A broad beach on the right offered the ideal lunch stop, and we pulled out sandwiches, trail mix, and pork rinds and sat back, paddling our feet in the water. I hadn't enjoyed a meal outdoors since Lewis's accident, and as the river whispered at my feet and the warmth of the sun caressed my naked back, I felt flushed with good feelings—for nature, for life, and for pork rinds, which I usually hated. The river was good, I remembered.

Soon afterward we were flying over ledges, punching through holes, sliding down sluices. We paddled past a dark rock that looked like a mountain gorilla. We picked our way through labyrinthine Stekoa Creek rapids the wrong way, ending up in a raft trap on the right, where the boulders closed in on us like a vault door. Rather than attempting to paddle back upstream to the correct route, we simply jumped out into the waist-high water, wrestled the raft over the boulders, and continued on our merry way.

On the South Carolina side we passed Long Creek Falls, which

made a cameo appearance in the film. Now it splashed its load into intense needles of light, hot enough to burn, and almost solid enough to pick up like nails from the surface. A turtle was sunning himself on a dark rock just beyond the spray, a crooked smile on his tiny face.

Not long afterward we reached Deliverance Rock, a medium-sized rapid where many of the scenes from the movie had been shot. Although a technical rapid with several maneuvers along the cross-grain of the current, it presented no problems, and we were soon at Raven's Shoot, named for the beaklike riverwide ledge, which we launched over as though in flight. The boulders were covered with moss and green lichens and contained a large amount of mica, causing them to glitter in the sunlight. In the quieter pools the mica hung suspended like gold flakes. We next snuck through the Tunnel of Love, where two boulders leaning against each another formed a small arch just wide enough for our raft.

We slopped over Last Supper, so named because it is the final rapid before the Five Falls section, a quintuplet of class IV and higher rapids, the worst section on the river. After we ate, we paused in a pool known as the Calm Before the Storm. The air shook from the sound of the rapids ahead—low-throated, massively frantic, and authoritative. We all exchanged looks and nods, then dug our paddles deep.

We plunged down a long stubblefield into Entrance Rapid, peeling from one side of the river to the other, crashing over a four-foot drop to the right of VW Rock. The fireworks had begun. We corkscrewed through the rapid of the same name, pitched over a pour-over, and bumped smack into the boulder barricade at Crack-in-the-Rock. We took the middle crack and fell over a five-foot falls into the beginning of Jawbone. The rapid growled at us, snapped its white fangs, and filled us with water as we slid past Decapitation Rock out of control. We had hoped to stop and scout the last pitch, Sock-Em-Dog, but we were too full of water to maneuver to shore, and the next rapid jumped at us almost immediately. It was the last rapid in the Five Falls section, and the worst—a funnel of water into which the whole river cramped and shot over a seven-foot drop into a nasty hole, blizzarding through the stones and beating and fuming like some enormous force chained to the spot.

"Paddle hard," I yelled over the thunder as we bolted down the spillway and crashed into the hydraulic. We were buried in whitewater, tons of it, pouring like cement from all sides. Under the avalanche, I felt a constant trembling of awareness in a thousand places that added up to a kind of equilibrium. When we shoved our way out, John Yost was missing from his perch to my left.

"Where's John?" I howled.

Heads spun in a frantic search. My stomach fell like a stone. We were in the recovery pool below the rapid. It was quiet, just the muffled roar of the falls behind. And no sign of John. I threw my paddle in the raft and dove in. John was my best friend. I had already lost one close friend to the river. I had spent months in mental preparation to rejoin the river, to accept what had happened as a freak accident, to reembrace the sport I had loved so much. Now, John was missing. It couldn't happen again. But it could . . . the river is totally implacable.

I dove in and probed with my arms. I was in a room of varying shades of green, beautifully graduated from light to dark, but there was no sign of life. When I resurfaced for a breath, John still hadn't showed. It had been half a minute. I thought the worst. Then, at the far end of the pool, downstream of our raft, just at the head of Shoulderbone Rapid, John surfaced, like a porpoise in a show. Water washed down his face, and he gasped for breath. We quickly paddled over and pulled him in. He had been stuck in the hydraulic, sucked down deep, and spit back up at the river's whim. He was fine, though, and not even ruffled by the close call.

"Let's get going," he grinned his famous cat-ate-the-canary grin. "This is what it's all about."

He was right.

There was a new tone in the river—an old one—something I recognized. We paddled through a few more small rapids before we lost our current in Lake Tugaloo. As we eased into the paralyzed water of the reservoir, hundreds of swallows flitted between us and the setting sun, making silver splashes as they dipped at the water. It was a pretty sight, but set against the ugliness of a constructed lake, where the quick life of moving water is choked to death behind a dam.

Ed Gentry, the protagonist in *Deliverance,* let such a lake bury three people, and with them the shame, the horror, the hatred he had encountered on the river. I would bury the same sentiments. For two miles we paddled across a landscape that evoked death: Debris littered the shore like skeletons. Stripped trees were bent over as though crying. It was here I saw the difference. The river upstream was a celebration of life, full of sparkle and exhilaration, brimming with beauty, bursting with challenge and the promise of attainment. This is what drew me to the river in the first place; this is what had called Lewis.

He had made a sacrifice, the supreme sacrifice, but it was in search of life, not sitting in the stagnant, polluted waters behind a dam or a desk. If only for a moment, he lived life to its fullest, rode along its keen edge. And I knew then he would want me to do the same. As we pulled our raft up on the bank, I turned to John and the others, cocked my hand over the blade of my paddle as though playing a banjo, and said, "What river do we do next?"

I was back.

36   **A** kayaker explores the depths of Crack-in-the-Rock (above), the third rapid in the infamous Five Falls section of the Chattooga. Large boulders block the river and form three slots over a five-foot drop. A paddler must remember to keep the paddle parallel to the long axis of the boat, or else it won't fit through. Right: The Chattooga and one of its tributaries, Long Creek Falls.

38

R. Harrison

Mishap in Cork-
screw Rapids.
*Rated IV–V on the
international scale,
Corkscrew is the sec-
ond in the spectacular
final section of rapids
on the Chattooga
known as the Five
Falls. After the movie*
Deliverance *was re-
leased, thousands of
inspired viewers came
to the Chattooga to
tackle the whitewater
featured in the film.
Some visitors had lit-
tle if any experience,
were improperly out-
fitted, and were un-
lucky: They capsized
and drowned in a
phenomenon that
came to be known as
the* Deliverance
Syndrome.

R. Harrison

39

Raven's Chute, on section IV of the Chattooga, one of the last free-flowing streams in the Southeast. Chattooga is a Cherokee name meaning place of the white rocks, such as those seen along the cliffs in the Raven's Chute gorge. The 50-mile-long river drops a vertical half mile through the Appalachian Mountains before it succumbs to the static waters of Lake Tugaloo.

Slim Ray

41

43

A t the Seven Foot Falls of the lower Chattooga (left), the current is split by a mass of boulders that force the river over a Wilt Chamberlain–sized vertical drop. Boaters who plunge too far to the right often encounter Alligator Rock, lurking just beneath the surface, eager to eat the unwary or unfortunate. Above: The kayak remains of one such encounter washed up on a rock below the Five Falls section, mute and flattened testimony to the savagery of the Chattooga.

January sunrise in the Chisos Moutains, Big Bend, Texas.

RIO GRANDE
Below Big Bend

It's the wild and scenic stretch."

"That's great," I enthused over the phone.

"It's not in the park, it begins just beyond the southeastern boundary," Mark Mills dryly continued.

"Oh," I was less enthusiastic to hear that. I'd always wanted to see Big Bend.

"But it is the most beautiful stretch of river, and it's really remote."

"Right. Can I fly to the put-in?"

"Ah, no. The only airstrip near La Linda is private. You have to fly to Midland/Odessa, then rent a car."

"Can I get a one-way rental?"

"No. You have to rent the car, drive three hours to the Gage Hotel in Marathon, leave your car, and pick it up after the trip."

"You mean I have to rent a car for nine days and just let it sit?"

"Yup. Like I said, this place is remote."

Mark Mills, owner of Outback Expeditions, was right. The Lower Canyons of the Rio Grande, or El Rio Bravo del Norte, beginning just beyond the park boundaries and continuing for 83-1/4 miles to Dryden Crossing, are remote, about as remote as you can get in the contiguous United States on a traveling adventure—that's what attracted me to the Rio Grande, certainly not its rapids or its wildlife. Its canyons are not the steepest or the most colorful. But it is bad-ass, backcountry remote. The few rapids that cut its course are given an extra point on the difficulty scale, just because the place is so out-there. If someone gets hurt, it's tough to get help or get out.

"Should we lose our boats, and escape the canyons, what chance for survival should we have in crossing these merciless, waterless wastes of thorns for a hundred miles or more to food and succor?" wrote Dr. Robert Hill on the eve of his 1899 expedition down the Rio Grande. Little has changed along the border river in the near century since then, though not far away civilization has swallowed the frontier like a small snake swallows a large horned toad.

The Rio Grande is also one of the few rivers in North America raftable year-round, though it is Dutch-oven hot in the summer months and can ice over in the winter. Fall and spring are the preferred floating seasons, and so I signed up for late October 1988. As directed, I flew into Midland/Odessa with photographer Pam Roberson and we met an old friend, Nick Reynolds, from my high school town, Bethesda, Maryland. We rented the car and headed south to Brewster County.

By early evening, we were checking into the Gage, an elegant 19-room, two-story, red-brick hostelry built by prosperous banker/rancher Alfred Gage in 1927. Walking into the lobby was like walking into Judge Roy Bean's parlor—copper pots, pigskin furniture, a leather trunk, a carved mesquite bullhead, handwoven cotton-and-wool saddle blankets hanging on the wall, spurs and sabers on the windowsill, a nineteenth-century pine bar that was originally a Mexican altar, and swords, blankets, and pots made by the Tarahumara Indians. The smell of saddle leather was in the air, and a group of cowboys, hats still firmly on heads, sat chugging Lone Star (the national beer of Texas) at a round table.

Giddings C. Brown, a former river guide, now the general manager of the Gage, met our little group, sat us under the tanned hide of an alligator splayed against the wall (a relative of Sobek, the ancient Egyptian crocodile god, no doubt), and ordered up a round.

"So, what's this area all about?" I asked, hoping for some good lies.

Giddings looked me square in the eye, saw my expectations, and said, "Big Bend is where all the lies you hear about Texas are true."

Here, too, we met Mark Mills, 30, the new owner of Outback Expeditions and our guide on the Rio Grande. Still vibrating from the frantic schedule of connecting airlines, renting a car, and driving at top speeds, I asked what time we would leave.

"Whenever," Mark replied. "No rush. Take your time. We'll leave when you're ready." He was operating on a different clock, and I wanted to switch to his time zone.

In the dry, crisp morning air where Marathon rides high in its 4,000-foot-elevation saddle, we loaded our gear into the Outback Expeditions' GMC Rally Wagon. We also met the rest of our party, Mike Edwards, 32, a trainee guide making his first trip down this section of the Rio Grande, and Sandy and Don Fielder, who lived nearby on a 40-acre ranch and wanted to try their new inflatable kayak on the river.

True to Mark's style, we eased through the loading process and didn't take off until late morning. We drove southeast across the Chihuahuan Desert, along the old Comanche trail, through the badlands of far West Texas, a thorn-incubating frontier with a lunar-looking landscape. In fact, the astronauts trained for their famous moon walk not far from here, and some still claim that actual event was nothing more than a film shot entirely on location in a secret corner of the Big Bend. Others insist UFOs make regular stops in the region, and the nearby Marfa lights—unexplained, ghostly pulsating balls of brilliance that make nightly appearances—are cited as evidence.

As I gazed past the odd cistern windmill to the barren blue and purple hills that were the heart of the Big Bend, I could almost believe that aliens would stop here for a picnic or some R and R. The Indians used to say that after making the earth, the Great Spirit dumped the leftover rocks at Big Bend. Now those distant rocks, some over a mile and a half high, looked like the montane equivalent of Oz.

The Big Bend is named for the sweeping arc made by the 1,900-mile Rio Grande around the Chisos Mountains after it rasps its way southeast from its source in the Colorado Rockies, through New Mexico, and down to the Texas–Mexico border. It's as though the mad river was touched with schizophrenia, and on the journey south, it suddenly changed its mind and partially reversed itself. With this crook the river acts as a gigantic moat entrenching the 740,000-acre Big Bend National Park on three sides. Actually, about 75 percent of the water that doglegs around Big Bend comes from Mexico down the Rio Conchos, a tributary about 60 miles upstream. So much water is diverted from the Rio Grande upstream that not long after El Paso it is reduced to a shallow trickle.

While the van trundled along, I browsed through Mark's library—books about the Big Bend region stored in an ammo box. One intrigued me. *How Come It's Called That*, by Virginia Madison and Judge Hallie Stillwell, gave a gossipy oral history of the place names we were passing.

"Is he still alive?" I asked about Judge Stillwell, who was described as the twentieth-century "Law West of the Pecos" on the book jacket.

"She sure is," Mark chirped. "Wanna meet her?"

Within minutes we pulled into the Stillwell Store, owned by living-legend Hallie Stillwell, the 91-year-old cowgirl. Mark steered the van next to a leathery gray-haired woman and asked if she was the famous Hallie Stillwell.

"No. You want Mom. She's inside." So Dadie Potter, 67, only daughter of Hallie, took us inside to meet the matriarch of the 22,000-

acre ranch we were on. Hallie met us with a sturdy handshake and clear look. She told us she had arrived in 1910 in a covered wagon and spent her youth, which still hadn't ended, roping steers, branding calves, and hunting. She once dropped a mountain lion with one shot from her Colt .45. And she was, indeed, a judge. In 1946 she was appointed justice of the peace, and though she never hanged anyone, she was as tough as Roy Bean and fined the mayor for speeding and revoked her grandson's license. In 1979 the town of Luckenbach held the "Honorable Judge Hallie Stillwell Hell-Hath-No-Fury-Like-a-Woman-Scorned Ninth Annual Chili Cookoff for Women Only." This lady was rawhide and silk, and as if to prove the point she pointed her shotgun at me and told me not to speed. I raised both hands and promised the yellow rose of Texas anything.

With an autographed copy of the December 8, 1987 issue of *National Enquirer,* which featured a profile of Hallie Stillwell, and some "Apache tears," tiny polished rocks that we bought from her store, we got back into the van and rode like the wind for the border.

At a little past one, we crossed the privately owned Gerstacker Bridge to the Mexican nontown of La Linda in the state of Coahuila. I was amazed there were no customs officials, no immigration procedures. There was nobody there. It was as easy as backing down my driveway and we were in another country. I made a mental note in case I might ever have to leave the country in a hurry and unnoticed. We bumped down a track alive with roadrunners to the edge of the great river.

It didn't look very grand. For 140 years, beginning with the Mexican War of 1848, this earthy brown liquid lariat has been the most tangible physical barrier between the United States and Mexico, as well as the symbolic frontier between the two dominant cultures of the New World. Still I couldn't help feeling vaguely disappointed as I skipped stones in one bounce across a waterway that would barely qualify as a creek in Brazil, India, and Zaire. Here it was the biggest thing around.

By midafternoon the two Miwok Riken rafts and the two inflatable kayaks were fully loaded, and we pushed out into the terra cotta–colored current. Waving good-bye to our shuttle driver, we drifted beneath the bridge, past a fluor spar–processing plant, then around the corner to Heath Canyon and beyond all traces of the human touch. I was suddenly filled with excitement. There was no whitewater, but I instinctively tightened my life jacket.

Mark let me row his boat while he paddled his Sea Eagle kayak, and it was a joy to pull on the oars once again after a year's absence. A slider turtle poked his thumb-sized head up and seemed to nod approval. The banks were lined with nearly impenetrable thickets of river cane, seep willow, mesquite bosques, and salt cedar (tamarisk). A windbreak im-

ported from the Mediterranean, the salt cedar had spread like a medieval plague, sucking up an unfair share of the water table. Beyond the riparian fence, the fluted walls (some crammed with the tiny nest condominiums of cliff swallows) slowly paraded past, and the river quietly rolled with barely a ripple. Some river runners, those in pursuit of hairball whitewater, would consider such a float a reduction of the river experience. But I had lived that phase, and now as we purled and I soaked in the silence, I felt the Rio Grande was in no way a reduction, rather a grand amplification.

After negotiating the furnace-winded Outlaw Flats section, we stopped for the night at a grassy meadow on the Mexican side, about 15 miles from our launch. The hunter's moon was near full, and as Mark went about preparing ocean perch, Vera Cruz style, I pulled out a bottle of the only appropriate drink for a first night in Mexico, Herradura Tequila, and mixed it with powdered orange drink to create Tequila Moonrises. Soddenly drunk and happy to be alive, we all collapsed under the cool light of the waning moon.

Morning brought the sight of Mike bent over a pot of coffee wearing a T-shirt announcing Perfect Student Body, and Pam agreed. Mark was sponging the rafts clean. I had never seen a river runner as orderly and tidy as Mark Mills and I would never have expected it on a muddy river in the middle of a desert. Mark had the oars on his raft marked left, right, and spare, and whenever we passed any semblance of trash, from tiny trot lines (cloth tags left by fishermen) to large Styrofoam coolers, he would paddle over and collect it. In my floating years I'd passed enough garbage to build Mount Trashmore, but I'd always been too lazy to collect it and had come up with lame excuses for my behavior. But in this canyon that lived by its own rules, Mark's fastidiousness seemed correct and inspirational, and by the second day I too was passionately involved in his private "Don't Mess with Texas" anti-litter campaign.

Now fully into river time, it was midmorning before we were floating once again. The pocked limestone walls, festooned with yellow rocknettle, began to reach higher. On the left bank was the Black Gap Wildlife Management Area, though the only evidence of wildlife we would see would be the muddy tracks of mule deer, javelina, ringtail cats, and beavers. The most exotic wildlife Mark remembers was a pile of South American pelts confiscated from a smuggling ring. On the right was Mexican ranch land, though there were no signs of ranching.

Our river guidebook carried a warning: "This trip is for properly prepared and experienced river runners only! It would be a very arduous and miserable trip for the careless or ignorant adventurer." In 1852 the Chandler–Green expedition released an empty boat at the top of a Rio Grande canyon, and nothing but splinters emerged from the mouth.

47

This sounded like a first descent of the Zambezi. At least it kept the crowds away, I thought, as we rounded a bend and came on a flotilla of canoes—the Blazing Paddles canoe club, a mixed group of overweight middle-agers who looked as though they had just parked their Airstreams and were spending the afternoon at the lake. Then within minutes two motor launches came roaring around the corner, carrying a group of beer-guzzling fishermen who looked as though they were heading for a chili cookoff. One of the paradoxes of praising the remoteness of a wilderness in print is that it will then almost inevitably cease to be so.

The day brought more of the same, quiet floating through stately limestone vaults whose walls were crenellated like the walls of a crusader castle. We ran two marked rapids, Big Canyon and Reagan, both rated class II but barely bumps in the road. Pam and Nick rode on my raft, while Mike rowed the baggage boat solo.

A big man bursting with energy, with a tattoo on his arm and a roguish grin, Mike had the trappings of the consummate river-god, except this was his first season rafting and his first trip ever on the lower Rio Grande. A former ice cream vendor, Mike had switched careers just a few months earlier when his freezer died. He had spent most of the summer guiding tourists down the popular 17-mile-long Santa Elena Canyon in Big Bend National Park. The one-day run features one rapid of consequence, Rockslide, which Mike had mastered, but beyond that he had no whitewater credentials. What he lacked in experience, though, he made up for with a knack for prevarication, a talent equally important in the river-god. As we floated down the river next to Mike's boat, the man spun yarn after yarn, tales of hoopsnakes and jackalopes, some of which I almost believed.

It was a long day, over 20 miles' worth, when we arrived at the bend just above a beautiful camp Mark had earmarked. But, as we drifted around the corner, ready for rest on a remote sand bench, we discovered the eyes of Texas were upon us—25 rafters in 12 identical blue rafts called Otters belonging to Bighorn Expeditions were parked in our space. Barely masking our indignation at being denied our manifest destiny, we waved at the group, big Texas waves, and continued rowing. Finally, just before sunset we arrived at the most famous rapid on the lower Rio Grande, Hot Springs, rated III–IV. There was a camp just below the rapids, one where we could soak our bones in a thermal springs, but first we had to get through the cataract.

A class III–IV rapid is respectable anywhere. The rating implies there's a reasonable chance of capsizing, and knowing that we were tired, that it had been a long day, that the light was quickly fading, and that this would be my first go at the rapid, I was a bit nervous when we pulled into scout. As I've done countless times before, I secured the bowline and

checked the rigging to be sure the raft wouldn't be swept away. And with a lump in my throat, I scrambled downstream to look at the challenge.

What I saw surprised me. Although the other rated rapids in reality hardly jarred the Richter scale needle, this one was touted as being major earthquake material, and the guidebook even showed a photo of a raft plunging pell-mell into a skein of whitewater. Yet, for all its press, Hot Springs was a lightweight, a simple class II drop down the middle. The only way you could screw up would be to enter too far left and then collide with a peninsular rock halfway down.

I was ready to take the plunge, but I looked across the Cañón de San Rosendo Creek, the one that had washed in the debris to create the riffle, and saw Mike staring intently at the drop. He looked frightened. Mark stood next to him and described a run with his finger, and Mike, puffing hard on a Kool, nodded quickly.

"Ready?" I yelled to them.

They both nodded yes, so I turned and headed back to the rafts. But not without stopping at 10-foot intervals and looking back to my mark, the entry rock I wanted to skirt to enter the rapid dead center. At the raft, Nick and Pam took their positions in the bow and off we sailed. The marker rock was easy to spot, we dropped down the tongue, glided over the first wave, buttered down the trough, bucked the last breaker, and with a couple of whoops we were through and parked in the eddy. Nick was ecstatic with the ride; Pam was laughing so that the band of gray in her hair fanned out like a comet's tail. They both jumped out to run back upstream to see if they could join Mike for his run.

I tied up the raft, pulled out my Minolta, and waded out toward the rapid in the half-light to see if my flash would reach Mike's run. Turkey vultures, those harvesters of death, were circling overhead. Shadows were staining the walls. Then in a quick minute Mike appeared at the brink, too far to the left. I watched as he entered the rapid, struck the first wave, which tore his oar from his grip and turned the raft sideways.

"Stroke!" I yelled from shore, seeing that a hard pull from his other oar could straighten him out for the collision with the peninsular rock just ahead. But, Mike froze, his tattooed arm limp. With a look of sheer terror, he sat motionless as the raft careened sideways into the rampart, rode up on its tube to the edge of a capsize, then snapped back, spinning the raft down the final pitch. It was over 50 yards before Mike could wrestle the boat to shore, and I ran down to make sure all was okay. Mike was shaken, his veneer cracked, pride punctured.

It reminded me of a run I'd made almost 20 years before, my first trip as a paid guide on the Colorado. When another guide became ill halfway down, I was given his pontoon raft with ten people to guide for the remainder of the trip. The first rapid I navigated was one of the easiest in the Grand Canyon, Ruby, yet I managed to hit its only exposed rock and tore a 25-foot-long rip in the floor of the raft. I felt as tall as a dung beetle and about as pure. Now, I knew Mike's trauma.

"Let me buy you a drink," I offered, but he just sulked toward camp.

Camp was not to be where we hoped. Yet another group had pitched tents around the thermal springs, so we made due on a sand spit upstream, across from a jagged cliff whose combed crest seemed to pleat the horizon. After dinner and a couple of evening ablutions in the form of Tecates, in the incandescent light of the full moon, Mike loosened up and started to take on his old sheen.

"Wanna tip?" I offered between sips.

"Sure, 15 percent," he cracked a smile.

"The most important part of running a rapid is the entry," I felt like the wizened Yoda passing on the secrets of the universe to the young Luke Skywalker. "Once in the rapid you're at the mercy of the currents. But, if you enter right, you've got it licked." That caught his attention. "And the best way to guarantee a good entry is to spot a marker wave or rock when you're scouting. Then when you walk back to your boat, every ten feet turn around and eyeball that mark, freeze it in your memory. If you don't, when you get into your boat and start the approach you won't recognize a thing, because the shore perspective adjacent to the rapid is completely different from the one from the middle of the river. That little technique can make a world of difference." It was such a simple system, but it had saved me scores of times, and now it somehow seemed like a piece of gold I was handing over.

"Thanks," Mike softly intoned. "Now, I wanna go run the Zambeanie." He meant Africa's Zambezi, which earlier I'd said I'd run. I couldn't tell if he twisted the pronunciation on purpose, but it didn't matter. Mike Edwards was going to be a river-god, despite himself.

In the moist coolness of the dawn, we took our towels downstream to the hot springs for a bath, but they were still too crowded with other boaters. As usual we were on the river long after the sun was baking the canyon and us. It made us lazy, which is the way you're supposed to be on the Rio Grande. For a time I even rowed with my eyes closed, listening to the descending trill of the canyon wren and the music of the reed section played by the currents.

We meandered past palisades of unconquerable beauty, past the scars of a proposed dam site, a private project that never got off the ground, thank God. We stopped at the Cañón Caballo Blanco for a hike up its sinuous chamber, past the whiplike ocotillos, the daggerlike lechuguilla, the blind prickly pear cacti (with its tiny barbed glochids that blind hungry livestock), and the polished Cretaceous limestone walls. Mark pointed out the candelilla, the plant whose wax has been smuggled across the border for decades to be used in chewing gum, phonograph records, shoe polish, and candles. Overhead, a hawk wheeled between the clouds and the international borders without passport or visa, while near eye level a Colima warbler flitted between cacti. We passed metate holes, Indian rock mills for grinding grain and mesquite beans. It was like walking through a diorama, and I half-expected a conquistador, a Comanche, or a Colombian to step from the shadows. At one point, I ran one hand across a hundred-million-year-old seashell embedded in the limestone, while I touched the petals of a day-old cactus flower with the other. Time, here, had turned to stone.

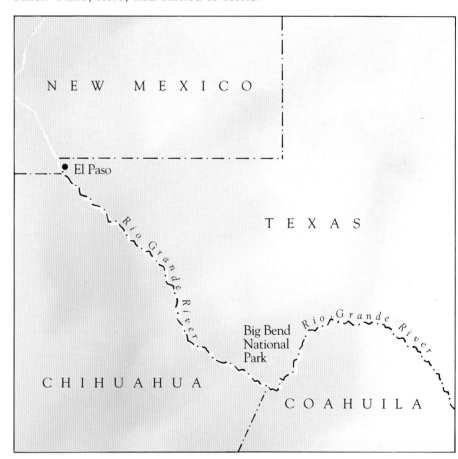

We only made 10 miles that day, stopping at Arroyo de Complejo del Caballo where Rodeo Rapids offers an afternoon of cheap thrills. More like a water slide than a rapid, the run is a series of safe interference waves that can be rafted, canoed, air mattressed, or swum without mishap. We tried them all, spending several hours at our private amusement park. This time no other creatures, human or otherwise, were around. For dinner we cooked up a 15-pound channel catfish that Sandy and Don caught from their inflatable kayak and sat near the whispering river under the great square of Pegasus and a ringed moon, indicating moisture in the air and perhaps rain.

49

In fact, the most dangerous aspect of the Rio Grande is not its rapids, not its poisonous critters, not even its remoteness. The most dangerous thing is its flash floods. They can come barrelling down a side canyon at freight-train speed and anything in their path will be swept to oblivion. The Rio Grande carries its threats of flash floods like a cocked shotgun. Now at the end of the rainy season, our guidebook reminded us repeatedly that 10 years ago this month, the greatest flood ever recorded on the Rio Grande roared through the canyon, killing wildlife and leaving debris in cracks 50 feet up the limestone walls, debris still dangling as an ominous warning of the power this river can unleash.

It didn't rain that night, but I had set up the tent near the rapid, and several times I awoke thinking the flash flood was coming, until I peeked outside and saw the river shimmering like mercury, a hauntingly beautiful sight under the full moon. In the morning, Mike showed up with a new T-shirt, Heart of Darkness River Tours, with a logo of a group of automatic weapon–toting rafters in silhouette. It was a not-so-subtle reference to the drug smuggling infamous in the area, and as if to confirm the message, over coffee we watched a red-tailed hawk chase a great blue heron; then the wedge of sky above the canyon filled with thunder, and a Drug Enforcement Agency four-engine AWAC plane with radar crossed our line of sight, followed by a twin-engine chaser. Maybe we were remote, but we were in the middle of a war zone, and the Rio Grande was the demilitarized zone.

Again we made a short day, running the other great rapid of the lower Rio Grande, Upper Madison Falls, rated IV, without a hitch. It made Mike feel good, and his chest was an inch extended as we pulled into Panther Canyon on the Texas side for camp. As dinner was prepared, we watched the last light play across the Sierra del Carmen Mountains across the river in Mexico, a sequence that took the cliffs from shades of pink to orange, crimson, deep rose, and finally dark purple. While we chowed down on tacos, black clouds rolled in and the moon darted in and out as lightning streaked. We heard the AWAC again, only this time it was nature speaking. In minutes the heavens broke loose, and a class V thunderstorm poured over our little encampment. Mike, Nick, and Don rushed to erect the Outback tents, while Mark battened down the kitchen, and I double-checked the bowlines. Everyone was thinking the same thing. Could this be the 10-year flood?

In my tent between lightning bolts, I thought about what to do if the flash flood did occur. I kept the zipper undone for a quick escape and figured I would make a sharp right and head up the highlands. I wondered and worried, until I slipped into sleep and awoke to a sunny and freshly scrubbed day. My lungs filled with the heavily perfumed air of greasewoods and creosote bushes. A millipede crawled across my rainfly. A blizzard of butterflies swirled through the mouth of Panther Canyon. Downstream, a gauzy mist hung across the river, and the walls above seemed to float in midair. It was as though we were experiencing earth's first morning.

Our last camp was at the labyrinthine San Francisco Canyon, on the Texas side. A nicer camp was across the river, but the Blazing Paddles had beat us to the punch, so we tented across the street and listened to their Bruce Springsteen tapes echoing across the canyons deep into the night, interrupted just once, by the drone of a large helicopter passing over us without any navigational lights.

On the final day whatever hold we had on the wilderness experience slowly slipped from our grasp. The canyon walls that soared for 2,000 feet just a day before now tapered to a tenth that height, the glossy limestone replaced by slopes of dull Del Rio mud. We passed an announcement rudely painted on a rock on the Mexican side: T. L. Miller, Jewelers, Odessa, Texas (Dick-Dolph). Then we passed a crossroads of sorts, as evidenced by the dozens of inner tubes, makeshift rafts, and a rotting door abandoned on the Texas side—the vehicles of illegal immigration.

We steered our vehicles down the last few miles. Nick Reynolds decided to paddle Mark's Sea Eagle to the finish line, and in the very last piece of troubled water, the lower part of Agua Verde rapids (a class II), Nick wrapped the kayak up against the wall and was ingloriously dumped into the river. Sucked down deep and held under for long seconds, Nick thought he was drowning and was embarrassed at the thought of his epitaph—Death by Drowning on the Rio Grande. Nobody does that. But, before his mind's eye got to the funeral, he had surfaced, and Don and Sandy had pulled him in like another catfish. He climbed back into his boat and arthritically paddled the final yards to Dryden Crossing, a junkyard with a take-out ramp. Nick was as depressed with his performance as Mike had been earlier.

Then Mike said, "Hey, we'll rename the rapid Reynold's Wrap."

Nick smiled, and the three of us, once remote and now connected in the flow of a common experience, helped tug the kayak above the high-water line.

"Let's do this again next year," Nick suggested.

"Yeah, on the Zambeanie," I countered.

And while throwing our heads back in laughter, we looked up to see a golden eagle disappear over the rim. The Rio Grande is as its name implies, but in ways never seen on the surface.

The Rio Grande near Solis Campground in Big Bend National Park.

Todd Jagger

51

52

Tom Till

*T*he Rio Grande near Boquillas Canyon and moonrise over the Chisos Mountains in Big Bend National Park. The Big Bend is named for the sweeping arc made by the 1,900-mile-long Rio Grande around the Chisos Mountains after it rasps its way southeast from its source in the Colorado Rockies, through New Mexico, and down to the Texas–Mexico border. With this crook the river acts as a gigantic moat entrenching the 740,000-acre Big Bend National Park on three sides.

Tom Till

53

Pamela Roberson

54

*T*he Yellow Rose of Texas, Judge Hallie Stillwell, rules over her 22,000-acre ranch adjacent to the Rio Grande, even though she's in her nineties. She once dropped a mountain lion with one shot of her Colt .45. With shotgun cocked, she warned Richard Bangs not to speed on his way to the river, or else. Right: Sunrise on the Rio Grande.

Tom Till

56

Pamela Roberson

Mark Mills paddling his favorite stretch of the Rio Grande, the Lower Canyons between La Linda and Dryden Crossing (left). The left bank is the Black Gap Wildlife Management Area; the opposite bank is the Mexican state of Coahuila. Right: Camp in the Lower Canyons just before a storm. The most dangerous aspect of the Rio Grande is not its rapids, not its poisonous critters, not its remoteness, but its flash floods.

Pamela Roberson

Camp in Granite Gorge, Grand Canyon of the Colorado, Arizona.

COLORADO

The River of Time

A stark descent through light and density and time is a float trip down the Colorado through the Grand Canyon. From the soft sandstones and flamingo limestones of the Kaibab Plateau, exposed at river level at Lees Ferry, the Colorado cuts through rock that progressively ages, hardens, and darkens. It plunges through the eons and the strata, through shales, conglomerates, and basalts, residues of primordial seas and cataclysmic eruptions and upheavals.

Until, at last, in the Inner Gorge, in the deepest corridor of the Canyon, the river washes against the oldest, blackest, and hardest rock of all: Vishnu schist. Dark as Dante's Inferno, almost 2 billion years old, the rock is a relic of a time when the earth's molten center disturbed its surface, imposing unfathomable heat and pressure that recrystallized sediments into new minerals. So dark it seems to swallow light, Vishnu schist is named for the Hindu deity worshiped as the protector, a syncretic personality composed of many lesser cult figures and associated with the sun. The rock, like depictions of the god, is dark-skinned and noble. From sandstone to schist, the voyage down the Colorado is one of dramatic change, a metamorphic journey. And like the peels of stone that compose the walls, the people who pass through the Grand Canyon change with each mile. They grow darker, harder, older. And some make the apotheosis to Vishnu himself.

I cozened my way onto the Colorado. Like any 18 year old, I was searching for the fantasy summer job, and when I learned people could get paid to raft tourists down the Colorado, I knew that was for me, my utter lack of whitewater experience notwithstanding. So, I fabricated a resume, listing rivers as intimates, although I had never seen them beyond a book or a slide show. My cover letter was as colorful a piece of creative sophistry as ever penned: Rafted 22 major rivers, guided professionally for three years, knew all the ropes (when in fact I couldn't even tie a bowline).

In 1968 the rafting business was barely that, but rapid growth was just around the corner. Bobby Kennedy had floated the Colorado with Hatch River Expeditions, the company to which I applied, and through the wizardry of Press Secretary Pierre Salinger, the story was a worldwide pickup. Between 1869, when John Wesley Powell made his exploratory voyage, and 1949, a grand total of 100 people had floated through the Grand Canyon. By 1965 some 547 people had rafted the Colorado; in the summer of 1972 the numbers had swelled to 16,432, and the Park Service stepped in and froze the use at that level. But in the late 1960s and early 1970s the wave of popularity was becoming tidal, and the few concessionaires servicing the budding industry had to find guides to meet the growing demand. My timing couldn't have been better, and Ted Hatch, the largest outfitter on the Colorado, hired me the day he received my missive.

Six months later I was circling over the Glen Canyon Dam, the 710-foot-high plug that creates 186-mile-long Lake Powell, before we began our descent into Page, Arizona, a town erected in the dust of nothingness to accommodate the dam workers. Within minutes I was standing in the parking lot of the Page Boy Motel, where I met Ted Hatch, scion to rafting royalty (his father, Bus, had pioneered many rafting runs in Utah and Colorado in the 1930s and 1940s). Ted extended a puffy, freckled hand in greeting, but he couldn't mask his disappointment as my skinny hand met his. Here he had hired a gangly, pale Atlantic seaboarder who appeared as guidelike as Ichabod Crane. But he rolled with it.

"You're swamping tomorrow's trip. We have the Four Corners Geological Society, one-hundred-ten people, ten rafts. Drive the winch-truck down to the Ferry as soon as you change out of that blazer and tie and help the boatmen rig. Welcome aboard, kid."

"Ahhh, one question, Mr. Hatch."

"Call me Ted. Now, what's your question?"

"What's a swamper?"

Ted reared his Cabbage Patch doll—head in laughter before explaining, "You dig the toilet hole at camp, help the boatmen cook, wash the dishes, bail the rafts. And assist the guides in every way. Now, get on it."

He handed me the keys and pointed to the truck. When I sidled into the cab, I knew I was in trouble—it was a stick shift. I'd grown up in an automatic suburb. I'd never even been in a manual. Still, I knew the basics and studied the diagram on the knob.

Holding my breath, I turned the key. It hummed. Fine. Toeing the clutch, I maneuvered the stick to the first position and the truck eased forward. Beautiful. I finessed across the parking lot, then headed down the motel driveway, a wave of pride washing over me. I slipped into second. No problem. Then, a thunderclap and plastic shrapnel sprayed the windshield as the truck jerked to a halt and stalled. Leaping from the cab, I ran for cover, finally looking back to survey the scene. I had driven the winch, which stood a good five feet above the truck roof, smack into the middle of the Page Boy Motel sign hanging above the driveway. The motel owner, with Hatch in tow, bolted to my side, issuing obscenities at a floodgate rate.

"Can you take it out of my pay?" I meekly asked my new boss.

"Forget it, kid. I'll cover it. But don't screw up again."

That was the beginning of a miraculous metamorphosis from sandstone to schist, boy to boatman, river ingenue to river-god. And it took its toll.

Somehow I managed to negotiate the truck down the 50-mile route to Lees Ferry. One of only two access sites for the length of the Canyon, it was named for John Doyle Lee, a Mormon fugitive who had ferried passersby across the river, after being implicated in the Mountain Meadow Massacre of 1857 in which 123 non-Mormon pioneers were murdered in southwest Utah. Lee was one of the first known non-Indians to find a new identity here, far from the persecution of Salt Lake City and civilization. Or so he thought. He was tracked down and arrested in 1874, apparently a scapegoat for the massacre, and executed in 1877. Perhaps progenitor to the waves of river guides who would come a century later, Lee was a man who had found his place in the sun on the river and was finally eclipsed because of it. He was also the Anglo embodiment of the fate of hundreds of Native Americans over the centuries—Havasupai, Hopi, Hualapai, Navajo, and Paiute—who had sought sanctuary and new lives in the rarified environs of the Grand Canyon, far from rival tribes, conquistadors, marauding white settlers, and Colonel Kit Carson.

Lees Ferry is now designated as Mile Zero of the 277-mile Grand Canyon experience, the launching pad for all river trips. It was here I took my assigned spot on the pontoon raft and held on as we pushed into the Kool-Aid green that passes for the Colorado, so colored since the silt settles out in the reservoir 15.5 miles upstream and the remaining microplankton refract their dominant hue. In the first mile I spun my head around frantically, taking in a view as otherworldly as a landscape out of a Frank Herbert novel.

As we passed into the buff-colored, cross-bedded cliffs of the Coconino sandstone and into the gates of Marble Canyon (not yet officially part of the Grand Canyon, that would come in 1975), propelled by a

20-hp Mercury outboard attached to the orange transom of our baloney boat, I desperately gripped a line, fearful that if I let go I'd be flung back to reality. We slipped into the soft red-and-maroon walls known as Hermit shale, clifftops soaring 2,000 feet on either side. The din of a rapid, sonorous and deep in timbre, thickened as we eased toward Badger Creek, named for the mammal shot by Mormon explorer Jacob Hamblin.

This was exciting. After six months of anticipation, of poring over picture books, I was on the lip of a major rapid of the Colorado. Glancing to the stern, where Dave Bledsoe controlled the tiller, I saw nonchalance unrivaled, a face fairly dancing with the aplomb of a centurion. As we slid down the coconut-butter tongue into the yaw of Badger Rapid and dropped into the abyss, the crisp 47-degree water slapped me and the pontoon pranced like a dolphin in flight. It was over in seconds and we pulled to shore to set up camp.

As we went about our tasks, erecting tables, filling buckets, clearing the beach of tamarisk (a loathsome weedlike tree encroaching on the beaches since the dam closed its gates in 1964, gates that denied the annual spring floods that once washed away such nonsense), Dave Bledsoe made a discovery—there were no paper plates. His veneer of pluck seemed to crack ever so slightly as he rifled the commissary boxes for a second look. "This is terrible," his words floated up the walls. "How can we serve one-hundred-and-ten geologists without plates. We need plates."

Seeing we were camped at the mouth of a tributary canyon (Jackass Creek), I asked Dave if it exited to a road, and if so, then perhaps I could hike out and fetch some plates. He thought the canyon emerged somewhere near Highway 89A, connecting Flagstaff and the North Rim. He figured I could hike out, hitch to the Hatch warehouse near Lees Ferry, hire a jetboat capable of traveling down to the lip of Badger and back to the Ferry, and get the plates to camp by dinner. So, with canteen filled, I took off up the twisting side canyon.

After an hour's hiking, the mazelike canyon divided into passages of equal size. Flipping a mental coin, I took heads, the left route, and continued. It divided again and again and again several more times. By the time I pulled myself up onto the flat plateau, I was completely disoriented, utterly lost. I could only guess the direction the highway passed. Kicking the red dust, passing a few Engelmann prickly pear cacti, I started east, away from the sun. But after half a mile I came to a sheer defile a hundred feet deep. Turning north, I came to another steep cut in the tableland. West, the same. It was Sartre-esque; there was no exit. Finally, toward the south, a spit of level ground streaked between two gorges and led to the shimmering asphalt of 89A.

On the climb out I had ripped my shorts, leaving a slightly obscene appearance, which didn't help the hitchhiking cause. It also didn't help

that even in rush hour this highway serves less than a car every quarter hour. Despite my frantic waves, the first four autos, all crammed with vacationing families, passed me by. Salvation came in the fifth, a Navajo in a pickup who delivered me to the warehouse, where I found several cartons of paper plates. I tracked down Fred Burke, who operated the Park Service jetboat, and in the waning light, we surged downstream.

As we approached Badger, I caught a queer sight on the right bank. On the spit of a sandbar, backed by a vertical limestone wall, a solitary man was hysterically waving his overshorts at us. Fred spun the boat around and picked up the marooned man, who stood on a few inches of dry sand that was disappearing as the river rose. This Daniel Defoe character was part of the Four Corners expedition. Several hours earlier when the group had stopped for lunch on what was then a broad beach, this Canyon Crusoe had decided to take a quick snooze behind a rock. He awoke hours later to find the cold Colorado nipping at his toes and the rest of the party gone. As one of the consequences of progress, the Colorado now rises and falls many vertical feet each day in an artificial tide created by the diurnal differences in electrical demands, flushing the four turbines that spin in the belly of one of the world's highest dams, Glen Canyon. In another hour, Crusoe would have had no place to stand, no place to go, save downstream, without a life jacket.

Reunited, just after soup, we passed out the plates in time for the salad and entrée. I was treated like a hero for my derring-do hike, and for the first time I had a sense of how it felt to be a river guide. The marooned client settled into the group little worse for wear, and I took my first repast in the Canyon.

I remember little of the next few days. As is not uncommon to first timers on the river, I picked up a bug and spent much of my time heaving over the gunwales or in delirium, collapsed on the duffel as we caromed through rapids, swept past unconformities, synclines, and other geological phenomena. At trip's end, I expected to be fired. I thought I had been a lousy swamper—sick for the majority of the passage, sluggish in my chores, not used to the harsh sun and physically demanding days.

But Hatch, in a moment of forebearance, kept me on. He assigned me to the boat-patching detail at Marble Canyon Lodge, a ramshackle motel near Navajo Bridge. For a month I lived the life of a desert rat, filling my days with Barge cement and neoprene patching material. Every few days another trip went out, and I stood aching at the Lees Ferry ramp, waving as the rafts dipped into the Paria Riffle just downstream. Out of boredom and desperation one afternoon, after uncovering a supply box filled with cartons of rotten eggs left from a previous trip, I drove down the Lees Ferry road and plastered each road sign with a battery of omelets. Waiting at road's end was John Chapman, the ranger, who

61

promptly sent me retracing my yellow trail with wire brush and soap and water. It took me two days to clean the baked-on eggs off the metal signs.

Finally, miraculously, a trip was departing that was short on help, and Dave Bledsoe requested me. This was my big chance and I hustled at every turn. I watched Dave's every move; I hung on his every word. His lecture hall filled with stories of hermits such as Louis Boucher, who operated a copper mine from 1891 to 1912, and of prevaricators such as "Captain" John Hance, who claimed to have crossed the dense clouds from the South Rim to the North on snowshoes. But the lesson that sunk in deepest was the history in the making, the story of river guides.

My ascension up the Hatch hierarchy was not mercurial. I swamped seven trips that summer—a record, I believe, before being made river guide. Some newcomers—Perry Owens, Jim Ernst—were piloting by their third trip. I wasn't disappointed, though. I loved the river. I lived for each trip and socked away my $20-per-day earnings while on the water.

Finally, on my eighth descent, I was given my badge and my own boat to steer. I was a River Guide. Now, peculiar things happened to me. My tan deepened, my chest filled out, my hair grew lighter and more lustrous. But beyond that, a heretofore unplumbed confidence surfaced and I found people reacting to me in an entirely different manner. At school I was undistinguished academically, athletically, socially. I was painfully shy with women and had never dared venture alone into a bar. But, on the river, everything changed. I brandished the rudder through the rapids, affecting that stern, purposeful look I'd picked up from Bledsoe. I lectured eruditely about the likes of John Wesley Powell and other explorers and about the deltaic sedimentary Hermit shale. I stirred Dutch ovens over the campfire like an outdoor Julia Child. People looked to me for guidance, wisdom, direction, political opinions, even sex.

That year I guided the president of MGM, a celebrated political journalist, the editor of the Chicago *Sun-Times*, writers from *Newsweek* and the *New York Times*, Broadway actors, television stars, successful professionals of every sort. I was in awe of these folks. I would never be able to speak with these people in the winter months, let alone eat, laugh, and play with them. But here they were in awe of me, kowtowing, following my every direction, hanging on my every word. It was sobering, unbelievable. When the president of MGM sheepishly asked me to help him set up his tent (he couldn't figure it out), I felt like the roaring lion in the famous logo.

And this was happening to every other guide on the river, every country-roughneck-cowboy-Vietnam-vet-farmhand who somehow backeddied into this nouveau elite club. At night, women—single, coupled, married—snuck over to the guides' sleeping bags under the cover of darkness. River romances were as common and flighty and full of trills as

canyon wrens. Back in Chicago, where I studied in the off-months, I couldn't get a date to save my life. But on the river, I couldn't find an evening alone. Klutzy romantics in December transformed to lusty Don Juans in June, and egos soared.

Most boatmen were quick to capitalize on this center stage and let loose bottled histrionics. They sang off-key before appreciative audiences, told bad jokes that sent laughter reverberating between the Supai sandstone, played rudimentary recorder as passengers swayed. Every guide took advantage of the rapids, all 161 of them. Those pieces of effervescence in the long, emerald band, formed almost exclusively by boulders washed into the main current from side streams in flood, were chances to shine, to showcase mettle and stuff, to enhance the legend of the dauntless river guide. Of course, the boatmen would never admit to the rapids' tendency toward impunity to visitors. Boatmen could flip, wrap, broach, jackknife, catch a crab, lose an oar, tubestand, endo, and swim the rapids and be relatively assured of emerging intact in the water below. But that was classified information.

All this theater was heightened in the late 1960s with the motordriven pontoon rafts. Nobody had yet figured out how to get through Lava Falls—the Colorado's biggest rapid and one of the last on the trip—with the engine running. The few attempts ended in broken shear pins, bent shafts, or outright loss of outboards, as the propeller invariably hit a rock soon after entry. So, two sets of 12-foot oars, unused on a typical trip, were lifted from their straps on the sides of the raft and mounted on the thoe pins marking the orange frame that gridded the pontoon's center. Then, the outboard was lifted and tied flat, like a roped calf, to the stern floorboard.

All the passengers walked around the rapid (Ted deemed the run too dangerous in those days) and watched and photographed in horror as two boatmen, one seated behind the other, entered the rapid, madly pumping the huge oars while being pitched and folded like laundry in the spin cycle. Then, as the last rooster tail was broached on the backside of the crest, the rear captain had to leap to the stern and, in a genuinely risky maneuver, pull out a knife, cut the ropes binding the outboard, pull the 80-pound motor up, slide it onto the transom mount, clamp it down, and pull the starter cord.

Time allowed just three or four chances to kick the engine to life (and it was sometimes too swamped to catch) in order to power the raft to a wisp of an eddy at the mouth of Prospect Canyon, where the passengers could reboard. If the engine didn't start in those few seconds, the raft would dive into the next rapid, Lower Lava, which was walled by a 75-foot cliff on the south bank that prevented passengers from hiking farther downstream. They would have to wait for the next raft and crowd onto it as it taxied them down to their carrier, waiting in a large eddy a mile downstream on the north bank. If the last raft in a party didn't make the critical landing or if all the boats on a trip were swept into Lower Lava—and this happened occasionally—the passengers would have to hike a half mile upstream, swim across the cold river, knowing that if they cramped they could be sucked into Lava, and then hike a primitive path down the north bank to the waiting rafts. Or they could wait for the next rafting company to come by.

All of this activity made a great show for those on shore. What I

soon learned was that rowing through Lava was really nothing more than a show. No matter what you did with the oars, be it snapping hard strokes throughout or freezing the blades in place, the results would most often be the same. It was, more than anything else, a piece of theater, and I learned to play it with Kabuki-like stagecraft.

This dashing, somewhat pretentious, rowing ritual was also employed, at some water levels, at the two other rapids rated 9–10 (the Grand Canyon has its own 1–10 classification scale for rapids): Hance and Crystal. A new addition to the fold, Crystal was created in December 1966 when a massive flash flood bulldozed a boulder-debris fan into

the river at Mile 98. But at the cusp of the 1970s, motor routes were being pioneered, many by Hatch honcho Dennis Massey, regarded by some as King of the River, the man who could make his raft dance in any wave, hole, or eddy on the Colorado.

Whether Massey or guides named Brick, Snake, or Bear, once below The Rapid, the boatmen would be feted as heros, hailed as Galahads, Lindberghs, champions charged with extraordinary backbone and bravery. Prior to my guiding, my only work experience was as a bellboy and carhop, and that didn't quite prepare me for idolatry. The river guides, me included, were exalted. The problem was some began to believe it, creating a duality in personality and self-perception, an almost schizophrenic state that was not easy to cope with or resolve. We were walking, rowing oxymorons. All of us relished those moments of Canyon adulation, but reality always returned at summer's end. Some turned to the slopes, some to carpentry or other crafts or service jobs. I went back to school. Still others dipped into the black books of summer's clients, those, who tugged from the beach after lingering embraces, said through tear-stained smiles, "Whenever you're in town, you must look me up. Come stay with me . . ." Following those words, many boatmen roamed from home to home, reliving the summer through slides, scrapbooks, and Super-8 movies and wearing out welcomes. But wherever we wandered, whatever we did, it seemed mundane by comparison.

The Colorado had irrevocably changed me, as it does everyone, fanned a false ego, then doused the fire. The boatman subculture was a strong one, a brotherhood bond formed in the summer months, and we kept in touch in the off-season, compared notes. Everyone seemed to suffer the same fate and searched in vain for a winter's equivalent of the astral light that caressed us in the Canyon. But no one found it. And we lived for summer.

For some, this game of ego Ping-Pong with its extreme highs and lows was too much. A bitterness developed that carried over to the arena of the river and was occasionally directed at the clients, the people who (it may have been subliminally felt) were responsible for building the granite pedestal in the back of the boat, then locking it in cold storage at season's finish. A boatman's attitude developed, usually after a winter or two of discontent, toward the clients quick with the swoon and compliments. These clients were *dudes* or *peeps*, with all the negative subtext swarming. Some of the veteran boatmen became cocky, smug, and elicited fraternity among peers at the expense of the clients. Others occasionally did something that hurt a client, mentally or physically. Often this was merely a personality clash or sloppiness or an honest mistake. Sometimes, however, it was spite and anger.

Once I watched aghast from shore as Dennis Massey steamed toward

63

Lava, full bore, without stopping to scout, without warning his clients, an impish grin across his face. The raft crashed down the boulder-strewn left side, crumpling like parchment, puncturing one tube, ripping the propeller off the outboard, and injuring three unsuspecting clients, including the Sierra Club leader of the trip, who broke two ribs.

There were many other incidents, all manner and magnitude, as the boatmen's syndrome spread and ran deeper. Of that first class of Colorado River guides, those who started in the 1960s with the evolution of the job into a livelihood and an identity, the adaptation success, the ability to resolve this external dialectic and live harmoniously with two opposing perceptions of self, has been mixed. Dave Bledsoe, after eight seasons as a river guide, left for Phoenix to repair air conditioners, the very ones that gulp power from the Glen Canyon Dam and give it cause for existence. Perry Owens, who started with me, died when he drove his sports car off a cliff in a drunken drive after an off-season party. Dennis Massey, fired after a series of passenger abuses, went on to become a pizza truck driver before he fatally shot himself.

Some guides adjusted quite well. They became doctors, lawyers, stockbrokers, even a politician. Others still run the river and wear the proud badge of river guide, perhaps now a bit faded from the harsh sun.

But whatever the path, once the silt of the Colorado had coursed through a boatman's veins, the hook was set, and whatever else happened, whatever activities came in-between, the river guide would rather be rafting.

A phone call came as I was writing these words.

"Remember me?" a distant voice queried.

"I don't know. The voice sounds familiar. Give me a clue."

"Molly Andrews, daughter of Peter."

And sure enough, something gave and a flood of memories rushed through. She was 9 in 1969 when her family boarded my raft for a passage through the Grand Canyon. Almost 20 years had passed and yet shared memories were clear as a tributary, crisp as yesterday.

"How about another raft trip?" she proposed.

"Sure, I don't need much of an excuse. A river guide once, always."

And I even recognized her at the airport.

Sunrise, Goosenecks of the Colorado, Dead Horse Point State Park, Utah.

John Telford

65

*D*ouble rainbow on the Colorado River. The river appears tamed and slight, but its scoured banks tell of a wilder time. Before the Glen Canyon Dam, the Colorado had surged along at speeds and volumes great enough to carry 500,000 tons of rocky debris and sediment a day, and during floods the daily tonnage had risen to 27 million. The river ran deep red, and it rasped into the earth like a file into soft stone.

66

68

John Telford

Gathering storm at the junction of Onion Creek and the Colorado River, Utah (above). *The summer storms in red rock country send flash floods down tributary canyons—floods that deposit thick silt and mud into the mother river. Right: At Mile 221, the results of upstream flooding show their colors. The Spanish named the river* Colorado, *for its brick-red cast.*

70

Liz Hymans

Considered by some to be the nastiest river beast in the West, Crystal was once a puppy of a rapid, barely big enough to wag a two-person raft. Then a once-in-a-thousand-year storm in December 1966 dropped 14 inches of rain in 36 hours and sent a flash flood down Crystal Creek that transformed the riffle at Mile 98 into the toothed monster of the Colorado—the rapid that flips more boats, sends more bodies flying, than any other.

Liz Hymans

72

Liz Hymans

The Colorado River experience has been described as hours of peace and serenity punctuated by moments of sheer terror and discomfort. Those special moments are not just found in the rapids, however. Weather can play a role. Cloudbursts are common in late summer, but what is lost in suntan can be regained in the camaraderie of the shared affair.

Sagara

74

Pat O'Hara

R edwall Cavern (left). A vaulting cave in the limestone formation of Marble Canyon. Major John Wesley Powell estimated that the theater-like chamber could seat 50,000 people. While the cavern might seat a third of Powell's estimate, it remains one of the most awe-inspiring amphitheaters nature has ever crafted. Right: Rest on Day 9 of an OARS commercial raft trip.

Pat O'Hara

76

Christopher Brown

Marble Canyon at Mile 45 (left). The limestone here is so smoothly polished that Major Powell mistook its true character. He wrote, "The walls of the canyon, 2,500-feet high, are of marble." Right: Havasu Falls plummets 100 feet on its race to meet the Colorado at Mile 157. The upper end of the stream waters the Havasupai Indian Reservation. Minerals in the water give the creek its blue-green cast and also produce the filmy curtains of travertine that hang from every surface touched by the falls' spray.

77

Larry Ulrich

78

David Edwards

Veteran river guide Dave Edwards reflecting on rock bosses and on his dirty job, knowing full well that somebody has to do it. Floating the Colorado through the Grand Canyon is a study in texture, color, and good complexions. The mud baths are free, as are the light shows.

Poppy Hill overlooking Ambush Rock on the American River, central California.

AMERICAN

Rushing Through Gold Country

The passage looked clean, down the middle between two greenstone-and-chert sentries. I pulled on the toylike oars, maneuvering through the waves, as both of us whooped with delight. But our revelry shattered as the rock partition on my right abruptly ended, revealing a foul-looking, basilica-sized boulder directly in our path. I tightened my grip and pulled harder, but the current had a stronger hold. We were going to collide.

"Do something!" Rick screamed from the bow. I thought maybe I could angle left and I got in a quick stroke, but immediately saw it wouldn't work. I tried pivoting to the right, but it was too late. We smacked the boulder broadside, and there was a sound like cracking rock. My right oar had snapped like a toothpick, the blade splintering into oblivion. The downstream tube started to ride up on the rock, and water began spouting in from upstream. The boat buckled and the frame cracked in two.

"We're going over." I looked into Rick's panicked eyes, and then saw nothing but foam and bubbles.

When we finally dragged our little raft to shore, we crumpled on the beach in exhaustion. After long minutes of silence, we took stock of the situation—frame destroyed, one oar gone, bottom of the raft ripped. The canyon surrounding us looked steep and isolated. There was nobody in sight. We hadn't seen a soul all day. Once, more than a century ago, this river had been packed with gold diggers. But they were gone and the river was now a lonely place to be. I was certain that the crowds would not be back. It seemed as if we were a hundred miles from civilization, from any sort of rescue. But we did have the spare paddle and one workable oar. We had to continue down the river. It was the American thing to do.

Back in the early summer of 1972 the South Fork of the American, in the breast of the California gold country, was still relatively unknown, a gem that a few daring souls attempted, enjoyed, and shared with friends.

I had been guiding the Colorado (my third season) and had heard about the golden run from a fellow boatman who hailed from northern California. He told me a guide named Bryce Whitmore had been taking Sierra Clubbers down this special stretch of river since 1963, but that it was still relatively unknown. He claimed it was the best of the West, technical rapids in a breathtaking gorge, and that someday it would attract thousands. If I wanted to see it before it became crowded, he suggested I hurry. I didn't believe a technical river could ever become popular, but he had whetted my appetite and I wanted to go.

The opportunity came early in the season. A charter group canceled, leaving me with a 10-day hiatus. I didn't own a raft, but fellow guide Peter Reznick did, a little sports car of an inflatable—a nine-foot-long, army surplus, cotton neoprene job. Peter had built a wooden grid frame and had purchased some dime-store oars. He loaned me the whole kit with a warning to be careful. Rick Szabo, my hallmate from college who had been swamping the Colorado that summer as well, volunteered to join me, which was great because he had a car and I didn't.

So, one Monday late in June, with the black raft crammed into Rick's trunk, we took off for California. Early Tuesday morning we turned off Route 50 in a place once called Hangtown, now Placerville, and briefly followed the Gold Road, Route 49, before taking a right turn onto Big Canyon Road. We found ourselves downshifting along a steep, winding road toward a fizzy band of water. When we reached the concrete Chili Bar bridge, we parked midway on the span, got out, and leaned over the railing upstream, welcoming the moist breeze on our cheeks. There was a sharp contrast between the cool, wet movement of the river and the harsh, hot immobility of the cliffs. The early sun striking the water made it look like hammered gold.

By the time the waters of the South Fork reached our view, they had tumbled almost a hundred miles from their source in tiny American Lake in the Desolation Wilderness area southwest of Lake Tahoe. I had gotten this from our road map and could also calculate that our projected take-out was about 20 miles away at Salmon Falls Bridge on the upper reaches of Folsom Lake, home of Folsom State Prison—the one that had Johnny

Cash singing the blues. Between here and there was just a blue line on the map.

We drove across the bridge and down to a gravel bar near the river's edge. No one was around. I jumped out, stepped over to the wild river, and stuck my hand in. It was chilly, snowmelt from the Sierra. This was Chili Bar, named not for the temperature of the water but for the Chilean miners who worked here during the gold rush. In fact, Spanish-speaking Indians were responsible for the river's wholesome name. Jedediah Smith had unimaginatively called it the Wild River, while fur-trapping the area in 1828. Many of the Canadian trappers preferred to cross the river at this spot, so the Indians named this ford *El Paso de los Americanos*. John Sutter took that name, anglicized it, and applied it to the river that flowed by his fort. In 1841 it appeared on a map. The name stuck and today remains the only river in the Americas named American.

As we pumped up our little vehicle, I surveyed the river. In the channel adjacent to our rigging, the hissing current rose like the back of a snake. I stared at the river for a long time.

"Three thousand cusecs," I stated flatly, impressing Rick. (The first lesson in guidespeak is cusecs or cubic feet per second, the volume of the river flowing past a single point.) I had absolutely no idea how many cusecs were flowing in front of my nose, except that this river was smaller than the Colorado and bigger than a creek.

The dry heat was rising as we shoved our dingy into the current. Rick squeezed his gangly body into the front compartment, while I sat high on the frame and took a mighty stroke with a pair of oars that felt like Pik-Up-Stiks. We had no idea what was around the bend, but we were soon in it: a long, choppy rapid with cleaver-sharp holes and slashing waves. The raft was full in the first few seconds, and as Rick bailed with our bucket, I flailed on the oars, negotiating back and forth across the river like Arthur Ashe playing full court on a set point. I found myself laughing uncontrollably, until I realized the rock at the bottom of the falls—the one that looked like a can opener—was dead ahead. I strained to turn the boat, pulling like a madman toward the left and nicking the edge of the granite rock. We spun into the placid water, cheering.

Our respite was short-lived, however. In less than half a mile the river's pace quickened; a cold wave snuck up from behind and slapped the back of the raft. It took off like a racehorse on a last-bend sprint. Rick hung on while I jockeyed for position, trying desperately to pull away from the wall where the current piled. But nothing worked and we slammed the cliff, then glanced back off. I had never seen whitewater this constant or steep. We were dropping 40 feet per mile; the Colorado through the Grand Canyon only drops 12 feet.

For the next couple of miles, we stayed pretty much in control,

82

dropping through some class II and III rapids without mishap. We passed massive exposures of slate, sandstone, and siltstone and tailing piles, remnants of midnineteenth-century mining operations. Beyond the banks the valley opened to low-rolling, golden-grassed hills, spotted with California oaks, pine, and scrub brush. We stopped at a large, clear creek entering from the south to turn the raft over and empty its load, and we found the evidence of a sawmill just upstream. Back on the river, the valley flattened pleasantly. A few cabins were tucked in the trees up on the slopes, but there were no signs of life.

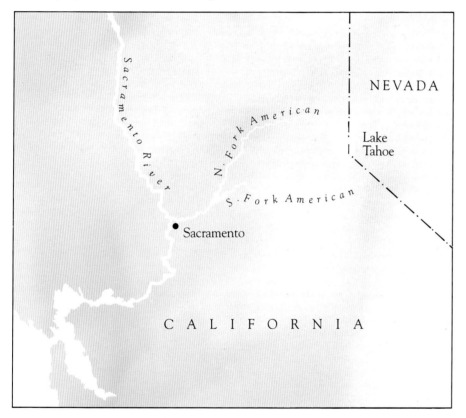

It was hot now, so much so the sweat seemed to stick like old grease. We needed another rapid to cool us off . . .

The river quickened its pulse. I strained to slow us down, but the river had us firmly in its grip and it dropped us into two consecutive troughs. Then just ahead it fell down a staircase, making a screaming right-hand turn into thundering water we couldn't see. The American was making us work. I pumped the oars, but I couldn't change a thing. The raft bucked and we crashed into a spouting, side-curling wave that kept us off the wall but threw us into a current-splitting rock in the final curve of the S-shaped rapid. Like a paper cup in a storm, we folded into the rock; a wave reached in and snatched away our bailing bucket. But we slipped off, swirling into peaceful water toward the Coloma bridge. Just beyond the bridge, we pulled in again to empty the raft at a place

where the river curled up against the shore. Turning the raft to drain, we wandered over to the full-scale replica of a famous mill, the one belonging to John Sutter.

After poking around for ghosts in the facsimile mill—there had once been 10,000 people living, working, and hoping here—we reloaded, swallowed the candy bars we'd brought for lunch, and shoved into the current. The river was listless, a torpid course whose bed had been gouged into giant pools by mining dredges. In some places the channel had been bent or straightened, water forced one way or another to expose the gravels that fed the endless appetite for gold. Now only the scars remained.

The river turned left abruptly, and we fell into the biggest rapid we'd seen yet, one that battered me around and made me feel old; and then we drifted some more. We passed under the Lotus Bridge, where the Gold Road wound up out of the canyon on either side. Just beyond were the twisted steel reinforcement bars of a previous bridge, destroyed in a 1956 flood that sent 72,000 cusecs bulldozing down the corridor.

At a class II rapid adjacent to an island, a dog stood foursquare on the right bank, barking his warnings like a mythological beast guarding the entrance to Scylla and Charybdis, so we eased down the left channel, continuing our odyssey.

We sailed through several more class II rapids, taking in water with every splash. After each, Rick frantically bailed with his hat, and I'd pitch in between strokes with my Sierra Club cup. The rock walls were becoming darker, evidence that we were in the Sierra Foothills Melange geologic zone, characterized by metamorphosed ocean-bottom sediment. And for a time, the river ran so quietly that we felt compelled to break out into song, bellowing "Old Man River," "Truckin'" (by the Grateful Dead), and "I Feel Good."

On the south bank we passed a granite boulder with a striped shirt stretched across it as though set out to dry. I rowed closer. It looked like something a convict might wear, perhaps an escapee from Folsom Prison, but tattered and faded, probably washed down in high water months before.

Then, off on the peak of a distant lemon-colored hill, stood a tree shaped remarkably like a lollipop. This tree was straight out of a Disney movie. And as we watched, the river swept us into the foul rock that cracked our frame, snapped my oar, and sent us swimming in the millrace.

Now we were faced with the prospect of getting downstream through an unknown gorge with a ripped boat, one oar, one paddle, and no bailing bucket. We jettisoned the remains of Peter Reznick's frame. I sat in the back of the boat using the oar as a paddle, while Rick sat kitty-

83

corner in the front with the ash paddle. We propelled our life raft into the night-colored granite defile, feeling as if we were the first to ever float into this constricting hell.

Far from it, 80 years ago, river drovers (the hired men who drove logs) rode sugar pines cut from the Georgetown Divide (a high Sierra ridge separating the watersheds) down the American to a mill at Folsom. They were the original river runners, piloting their crude rafts without life jackets or first-aid kits, or whiny clients. The logs often jammed at the narrow gorge we were in, and so the owners of the American River Land and Lumber Company used tons of black powder to clear away any obstacles. They couldn't clear them all, such as the foul rock that had capsized our boat, but they did improve the passage, perhaps to the degree that would allow rafting in the 1970s.

But we didn't know that as we rode up on a haystack and then toppled into a rapid that spun us around as though we were in a whirlpool and sent a lateral wave pounding over our heads, washing away our chief bailing apparatus, Rick's hat. That left my Sierra Club cup. I frantically pitched water from our bilge. But I was getting nowhere—the rip in the bottom of the raft ensured that. I was so intent on my bailing that I didn't notice we were dropping into another rapid.

"Paddle right!" Rick screamed.

But my oar was somewhere in the bilge, so I stuck my cup in the river and tried to help. My efforts in the drop were useless. On and on we tumbled, riding more haystacks, bouncing off rocks. In one left-bending rocky chute, I was pitched to the bow and cracked my head against the back of Rick's.

"Where's the hospital?" I moaned.

"Where's the bar?" he asked as we recovered in the next rapid.

Soon after the river curbed its punishment, slowing to a slug's pace, and we could see the telltale chalklike streaks of lake-level water on the walls. There was one last disturbance, a steep, sharp bend to the west, and we were in the backwaters of the reservoir.

"Where's the champagne?" We looked at one another with tired grins, rubbing our rubbery limbs and bruised shins.

It was an awkward, tedious process to paddle the limp, half-filled raft across the final mile of stagnant lake water in the slanted light of late afternoon. But we were thankful to be alive, to have survived. We beached at Skunk Canyon, and as we pulled ourselves up to Salmon Falls Road to hitchhike back to Rick's car, I turned and looked back down at the now-quiet waters of the South Fork of the American.

"What do you think?" Rick asked, seeking some pearl of truth from me, the Colorado veteran.

"It'll never catch on . . . too rough, too remote. It almost killed us.

It's too dangerous to ever be a popular river run."

Rick nodded in agreement, and I felt smug in my assessment as a pickup truck slowed to give us a ride.

Less than 10 years later the South Fork of the American would become the most popular river run in the West, with over 100,000 boaters a summer and some 79 licensed outfitters. David Bolling, an executive director of Friends of the River, would call it the "K-Mart of California rivers: nineteen miles of low-budget whitewater with easy accessibility, plenty of parking and hordes of consumers shopping for cheap thrills." On some summer weekends, the river would be wall-to-wall rubber, and traffic would gridlock above the rapids.

Troublemaker Rapid, the one where we lost our bailing bucket, would be declared the "single most popular rapid in America." There, and at other raft-twisting rapids, commercial still and video photographers would capture boaters in their thrilling moments on film and tape, and then hold up a signboard with the number of the shot so it could be purchased at trip's end. Outhouses and picnic tables would line the areas reachable by road. A seven-mile stretch of cabins, trailers, and stately homes would be designated the El Dorado County "Quiet Zone," and boaters were supposed to whisper reverently when passing through.

It is now a far cry from the wilderness experience Rick Szabo and I shared in the summer of 1972. Yet popularity has not ravaged the river, only my reputation as a seer. Rather it should be credited as having saved one of the most remarkable rivers in the country. The hundreds of thousands who have floated the South Fork have felt its specialness, have been caressed by its waves, have witnessed its beauty. They have lent their support and their passion to fight the dams and water diversion projects that have been proposed over the years and will continue to be proposed on any stretch of free-flowing river in the world.

The American has become like the mandate of its namesake, a melting pot that services all without regard to race, creed, or paddling ability. The young and the old, the diamond-studded and the barefoot, the powerful and the disabled have all floated the South Fork of the American, soaked in its sun, and beamed with its pleasures equally. There is nothing more democratic than a paddle boat and little outdoors that is more fun.

And when the time comes to rally the troops against the hydropower mongers, the constituency is built-in, baptized, and ready for action. For now, the state legislature has guaranteed the river temporary protection. The more people travel this stretch of river, the less likely that status will change, and the great American adventure will be available for generations of Americans to come.

The American is a precious gem running through the heart of the gold country.

86

Liz Hymans

Tunnel Chute at Mile 2.5 on the Middle Fork of the American River. The tunnel blasted by miners through a narrow ridge is flat and easy. But the dynamited chute leading down to it has sharp sides that can rip rafts and kayaks and ends in a big drop with a powerful reversal. Many trips prefer to portage.

Liz Hymans

Liz Hymans

The biggest rapid in the infamous American Gorge (rated III +), Satan's Cesspool, also called Lost Hat, is at Mile 16.9 on the South Fork of the American. At the end of a long pool, the river pours over a sharp drop then bends left and right into a bigger back-curling wave drop against the left wall. After the encounter with the devil's own, the aptly named Dead Man's Drop waits just below.

Liz Hymans

89

The American is literally a river of gold. On its
banks in 1848, James Marshall discovered gold
in the tailrace of Sutter's mill. His find launched the
great Gold Rush of 1849 and poured fortunes into
San Francisco, Sacramento, and the entire state.
Today, fortune hunters still pan the cobbled river
bed, and passing river runners can still hear cries of
"Eureka" as the occasional nugget is gleaned.

Photo above by Liz Hymans, large photo by Christopher Brown.

The Rogue River just below Rainie Falls, Oregon.

ROGUE

Scoundrel of the Pacific

Alternately tranquil and tumultuous, the Rogue chisels through the bristled plateau of the Siskiyou Mountains, taking on the character of a coastal river: a steep-sided, narrow, and heavily forested canyon with moody, molting pools and sudden, spuming chutes and rapids. The French trappers who worked this watershed in the early nineteenth century found the waters troubled, but the Takelma Indians more troublesome, and so they called the river *Les Coquines* ("the Rogues") after their local adversaries. A century and a half later the Rogue would prove a rascal of a river for me as well.

When television producer Ron Roth walked into my office in the California gold country, he said he was looking for a whitewater river.

"You've come to the right place," I beamed. A half dozen such rivers tumbled down the western slope of the Sierras within a couple of hours of Angels Camp. "Exactly what kind of whitewater river do you want?"

"It has to be terribly wild, terribly scenic, with big rapids, big trees, and great restaurants."

So, I hopped into Ron's El Dorado rental car and we toured the mother lode for the next couple of days, driving to the Stanislaus, American, Tuolumne, Mokelumne, and Merced rivers. Then we flew over some more. And we ate at some great restaurants. But no matter what I showed Ron, he never seemed satisfied.

"It's just not right," he kept mumbling. Finally he left for Los Angeles, promising to give me a call.

Right, I thought.

But he did. Three months later. I had practically forgotten our Sierra circuit.

"We found the perfect river for our film. It has everything. It's the Rogue."

The Rogue River in southwestern Oregon rises in the Cascade Range, northwest of the royal blue waters of Crater Lake, at about a mile above sea level, and makes a 200-mile dash to the Pacific. After spilling through spectacular and pristine timberland, it drops into the broad, fertile Rogue River Valley, where the farms and orchards around Medford and Grants Pass are often clouded by haze from lumber mills, the economic underpinning of the region. Below Galice it picks up speed again, spinning its waters through one of the most magnificent wilderness corridors in America. Then it pauses before making its final exhale into the sea.

An 84-mile section of the Rogue was one of the first eight rivers (known as the Instant 8) designated as part of the National Wild and Scenic River System in 1968. The river earned its initial fame as an angler's paradise for anadromous (sea-going) fish and has been called "the fishingest river in the West." The late spring chinook salmon run and the early fall steelhead trout run attracted fishermen from around the world. Others were lured by the writings of Zane Grey, who had a cabin on the Rogue during the 1920s and 1930s at Winkle Bar.

In the middle 1960s, however, some local outfitters and an ever-increasing number of private boaters discovered the Rogue as a fine river to run for its own sake—for its rapids, wildlife, and scenery. At the same time it attracted Hollywood. Debbie Reynolds went barreling down the Rogue on a log raft in *How the West Was Won*, and John Wayne and Katharine Hepburn did the same in *Rooster Cogburn*.

I knew the Rogue only by reputation, and it was a river I ached to run.

Ron Roth was clearly pleased with his choice and, in a moment of joy, invited me to join the production as the whitewater stunt coordinator and a stunt double for two of the lead actors. Somehow in the excitement he neglected to ask whether I had ever been down the Rogue, and I sort of forgot to volunteer that information.

The film was to be called *Killing at Hell's Gate,* a CBS Movie of the Week, starring Robert Urich, Joel Higgins, Deborah Raffin, and Lee Purcell. The plot was a watered-down *Deliverance*. A congressman seeking favorable publicity embarks on a river trip. The river he chooses has recently had its wilderness classification enlarged, which effectively closes down a large lumber mill. Of course, the congressman voted for the extended protection for the river corridor.

Accompanying the congressman are his sexy aide (naturally), a Jus-

tice Department lawyer (our hero) pressed into service since he hails from the area and has planned a reunion vacation there, the lawyer's high school buddy who shares a birchbark (ahem) canoe with him, and a stunning female raft guide who operates the congressman's raft. Everything appears to be the picture-perfect Washington perk weekend until three now-jobless employees of the lumber mill out drowning their misfortunes in alcohol spot the entourage coming downriver. In their spiteful stupor, the mill workers attempt to shoot a vengeful hole in the congressional raft; they miss, killing the congressman.

Since the killers know they were seen by the survivors, they figure the other four must die as well. And the hunt is on.

As bullets fly and darkness envelops the river, the lawyer's boyhood friend attempts a daring nighttime run of one of the Rogue's worst rapids, Blossom Bar, hoping to make it through and return with reinforcements. His attempt fails, of course, and in true Hollywood tradition the lawyer dives in and tries swimming through the rapids to safety.

I was to be the stuntman who would steer the solo canoe through Blossom Bar and swim the rapid as well. My first job, though, was to recruit professional whitewater guides to act as stunt doubles for the key characters. They had to be pretty much the same size and shape as the actors. Breck O'Neill, my long-time friend, was hired directly by Ron Roth to be the Robert Urich double paddling the front of the birchbark. Breck had worked with Ron a few years before on another film, *The Mighty Niagara.* Though an experienced rafter, Breck had never paddled a canoe—a fact he didn't tender to Ron. For much of the shoot I was to double for Joel Higgins, playing the lawyer's buddy, in the stern of the canoe.

I recruited veteran guide Joan Reynolds to play Deborah Raffin's character, Anna Medley, the beautiful raft guide. Tall and striking, Joan fit the part, though she had to wear a blonde wig over her raven hair. I offered the role of the congressman (played by Paul Dooley) to Steve Merefield. Steve refused when he heard he would have to cut his shoulder-length hair, until he heard what the day rate and the bonus for falling in the river after getting shot would be. His locks came off pretty quickly. The last double I needed to recruit was for the congressional aide, Lee Purcell, who was five foot three inches and 100 pounds.

Try as I did, I couldn't find a woman guide that tiny. A few days before shooting was to begin, I called Joanne Taylor, an Angels Camp waitress I had dated.

"You want to be in the movies?" I proposed in my best imitation of a Hollywood producer. She was skeptical. Although she had the correct dimensions, right down to jeans and shoe size, she had never even been in a raft and couldn't understand how she could be hired as a professional whitewater stuntwoman without having better credentials.

"It's easy," I countered. "You're supposed to play a secretary on her first raft trip, an indoor type out of her element, scared to death of the water. Just be yourself, and the producer will think you're brilliant."

A week later we were ferried upstream in flat-bottomed, aluminum hydrojet boats to Paradise Lodge, not far below Blossom Bar. This would be our base for a week of shooting.

The Rogue was gorgeous, beyond my expectations. Rusty-red bluffs, topped with Pacific madrone and Oregon white ash, loomed 400 feet above the river. The lodge grounds were bordered by giant-leaved Indian rhubarb, salal, salmonberry, and scarlet California fuchsia. The Mesozoic Era canyon walls featured streaks of serpentine and greenstone. A black-tailed deer wandered near the foot of my sleeping bag the first night, and in the morning the mist curled through the Douglas fir. Ron was right. It was the perfect river.

The first few days we shot the main actors exchanging dialogue in the flat water below Blossom Bar: "Canoes and rivers are like men and women . . . they can be dangerous, but what's the choice?" "He sewed a girl to a mattress . . . doesn't have both paddles in the water." "When we get into the rapids, the fluffy white stuff, it looks soft, but it can float a brick."

In the off-time, I taught Bob Urich and Joel Higgins how to paddle the canoe, a 15-foot aluminum Grumman painted by the prop department to look like birchbark, even though birch doesn't grow within 2,000 miles of the Rogue. And some long shots were taken of our stunt doubles paddling through riffles. Joanne Taylor, who awkwardly gripped her paddle like a broomstick, looked appropriately scared and green. It was all easy, lucrative, and fun. Then, it came time to film the hairball action; the stuff the director, Jerry Jameson, said would "put *Deliverance* in the archives." And that was up to me.

I was the first one up to Blossom Bar that morning. I had about two hours to scout while the jet boats ferried the rest of the crew to the site.

I was looking at a river in spring-runoff spate. The rapid, named for the wild azaleas along its banks, looked like a rock garden gone to weed. It was a slalom course of water-sculpted, house-sized rocks, with a tricky zigzag route down the middle. But the director didn't want me to go down the middle. He wanted something more spectacular—a run down the boulder-choked right bank near where the cameras would be set up.

Until 1930 Blossom Bar was so clogged with boulders, there was no passage. But then legendary riverman Glen Wooldridge blew the worst rocks out of the water. His demolition strategy was simple. He filled a gunnysack with dynamite and stones, worked his skiff up behind an offending boulder, lit the fuse, dumped the bag, and then rowed like crazy

downstream. Now I wished I could do the same, since the route Jerry Jameson described to me was one ole Glen had left intact.

The scene was to be the pivotal disaster of the film. The congressman had been shot and killed, and the survivors had spent the day crouched behind a protecting rock while the killers stalked them from the canyon rim. With the cover of darkness, the Joel Higgins character says he'll go for help by paddling the canoe solo through the worst of Devil's Gorge. The script describes him running a series of increasingly difficult rapids, until he pitches over a waterfall and capsizes. It sounded terrific on paper, but in reality Joel Higgins would watch from shore while I tried to flesh out the part.

Nervously, I paced the banks as the crew set up the cameras. The route required threading a needle through various boulders, then dropping off a waterfall into a hydraulic—a nasty piece of recirculating water that could hold a boat or a boater for days. The cameras would be shooting "day for night," meaning the lenses would be stopped-down so daylight would appear as night. I figured that meant I could take a little liberty with my appearance in the scene, and as I suited up I slipped on an extra life jacket under my lumberjack shirt. But, the director said it made me look too fat—I'd have to use just one. Joanne Taylor overheard the conversation and afterward took me aside to entreat me not to go. Then I knew I had to.

When the director waved for action, I eased the canoe into the current, pointing the fake birchbark bow toward my destiny. A great blue heron disturbed by my presence flapped its wings and took off like a pterodactyl upstream, the direction I would have preferred. My throat was so dry it felt as if it were cracking. A primitive fear shot through me, but I was committed and kept paddling.

Then I was in it, sliding down the apron strings of the rapid, racing past the granite markers and over the waterfall, into the angry hydraulic where I braced for the capsize. Instead I emerged right-side-up, intact, barely wet—the script called for a disastrous capsize. Thinking quickly, I grabbed the gunwales and pulled the canoe over in the relatively calm water just below the falls, then flailed my arms and legs as though being attacked by Bruce the shark.

"Cut! Cut! Cut!" I heard the director scream as I surfaced. There was no applause as I pulled myself onto shore. Ron Roth took me aside. He said the director wanted to send out for professional stuntmen, but he wanted to give me another chance. I had to capsize *in* the falls and I had to cut down on my theatrics in the water, or else I'd be replaced.

As I walked back up to try again, Jerry Jameson cornered me. "Look, son. Don't overact once you're in the water. Look at the way Joanne does it. She's a pro like you, but she comes across on camera as

95

though she's inexperienced and frightened, and she does it without all the hoopla. Follow her example. Cool down a bit."

With those words ringing in my ears, I launched downstream. "Act like Joanne; do as she would," I mumbled my mantra. Then I was in it. I tried to make the run sloppier. I grazed some of the beginning rocks. I lined up off-center to pitch over the worst of the waterfall. But as I careened into the hydraulic, I could feel that the canoe was too stable—that it just wasn't going to capsize. Only this time I knew it sooner, so before I emerged, I snatched the side of the boat and pulled it over under the cover of whitewater. Once in the water I tried to panic, but not too much—just like Joanne.

"Cut!" I again heard from shore, but this time the crew clapped as I pulled myself from the water.

"Nice job," the director said. "Still a bit melodramatic, but it'll do."

And we were on to the next scene.

Now I played Charlie Duke, the Bob Urich character, who decides to swim the Rogue to safety when Joel Higgins never returns from his midnight canoe trip and the remaining raft is punctured by a bullet. The swim was through a more forgiving piece of Blossom Bar, but again it took several takes for me to tone down my acting and get it right.

Then a real drama occurred. Between takes of my swim, a commercial raft slopped down the left-hand side of Blossom Bar and struck a large obstructing boulder sideways. The raft "wrapped" around the boulder as if it were a giant pancake plastered against the wall. The crew scrambled up onto the boulder's dry crest and frantically waved at another commercial raft heading into the rapid. The film crew stopped its activities to watch the sideshow as the second raft caromed through Blossom Bar toward the wrapped raft. It too approached the boulder broadside and suddenly wrapped, this time folding around the first raft. The crew of the second raft scurried to the crowded roost atop the boulder, and now both sets of marooned crews waved hysterically at yet another approaching raft.

The oarsman of this third raft could see the expanding obstacle in his path, and he positioned his bowman with a throw-line that could be tossed to the stranded crew as the raft slipped past the aerie. Yet as he negotiated to get close to the dual shipwreck, he miscalculated and slammed into the jam, turning the situation into a Triple Wrap, a phenomenon I'd never before heard of, much less seen.

This was great theater for the professional showmen from Hollywood, but Joan Reynolds saw her fellow river guides in trouble and wanted to help. She stormed over to the director and demanded that she be allowed to take one of the production rafts across the river with some of the propmen and grips to help in a rescue attempt.

"No. Out of the question," Jerry Jameson spat back. "This production costs over $100,000 a day. We can't stop to get involved in a rescue attempt. Nobody's hurt over there. They can figure out how to save themselves. We're a big production . . . we're more important than the fate of a few river rats."

Joan was so upset that she threatened to quit. But she said she needed the money and grudgingly agreed to stay. It struck me that this little drama mirrored the theme of the film, which was exploring (albeit superficially) the conflict between the larger good of the planet and all human beings and the immediate needs of a small number of people. In this case, the congressman had promoted legislation that would preserve the Rogue River region as a wilderness for generations to enjoy as a temporary refuge from an increasingly pressure- and people-filled world.

Few argue that such wilderness is necessary to ensure the sanity of our species and, perhaps, to keep the fragile ecology of the planet in check. But preserving this one corridor shut down the lumber mill that put bread on the tables of dozens of families. In the script some men had worked at the mill for decades and were suddenly faced with unemployment. Their livelihoods were sacrificed for the preservation of the surrounding forests and, in the short term, for the enjoyment of wealthy tourists who would fly into the region for a weekend of rafting.

As the congressman says around the campfire after his first day of rafting, "It's this putting aside certain areas to protect the wilderness . . . that's what it's all about . . . to keep it wild and free. I care about those men and their families. I know what a paycheck means to them. But I would like their children and their children's children to be able to come out here and enjoy this treasure."

Somehow this conflict, which is the essence of most environmental issues, came into play here in a corrupt, convoluted form. We were witnessing the personal tragedies of three raftloads of vacationers. They were stuck. They weren't in real danger; it was more embarrassing than anything else. Still, they had a problem, but the larger concern, the "important film" driven by economic forces, took precedence.

So it becomes a question of degree. In preserving a wilderness area, how many lives should be allowed to be ruined through unemployment before the human sacrifice is not worth the long-term benefits? How many people must become marooned, or how severe must their danger be, before the film company stops filming and helps? Would production stop for an injury? For a death? There is no script for real life.

With an eye on the stranded rafters, the production went back to work. One by one the rafters jumped into the water and swam through the rest of the rapid, making it to shore without apparent mishap. And at the end of the shooting day, when the director yelled, "It's a wrap," meaning that the shooting was over for this part of the film, we couldn't help but snicker.

As we boarded the jet boats for the trip back to Paradise Lodge, two of the three shipwrecked rafts had been freed, loosened by crew members pulling with lines from shore. The third, however, remained like a postage stamp glued to a granite package.

Next the entire crew moved its base to Grants Pass, with several days' shooting in the short but steep-walled Hellgate gorge, a passage with no dangerous whitewater and easy access for the film crew. In order to make it look as if the actors were really running the rapids, we tied their boats to a raft that Breck and I steered through some riffles. The cameraman, Bill Butler, took tight shots of the stars from the steering boat, with splashes and bits of swiftly moving bank in the frame. Then that footage was cut into the long shots of the stunt doubles actually shooting the rapids. That was next on our agenda.

While the director and actors went off to film the scenes that took place off the river, the five stunt doubles were given two sets of matching clothing, a list of needed shots, and directions to be back in five days. Roger Brown, the legendary director of adventure documentaries, accompanied us in another oar-powered raft.

We put in at the traditional start of the commercial tour—Grave Creek Bridge, 650 feet above sea level, near where the daughter of a pioneer couple was buried under an oak tree in 1846. I was concerned about running the Rogue in an open canoe fashioned to look like a birchbark with Breck, a canoeing novice, as my bowman. I had quietly told the propmen several days before and they produced a specially designed canoe, assembled in Hollywood, filled with high-flotation ethafoam, except for the compartments where the paddlers knelt. It was, in fact, a supercanoe—something that Q would design for James Bond. The thing was weighted like an inflatable punching doll. If you tried to turn it over, it would roll back up in a snap.

So, dressed like the stars of the movie and piloting our supercanoe, we headed down the wild and scenic Rogue River. The first rapid, Grave Creek, immediately below the bridge, tested and proved the seaworthiness of our vessel. The first wave washed over the high crescent of the ersatz bow and rolled back to slap me in the face. Another followed and another, action that would have swamped a lesser craft. We sailed through without a hitch. A couple of fishermen on shore stared at our unlikely progress in amazement.

After a mile and a half of quiet paddling, we came to the notorious Rainie Falls. We pulled in on the left bank, tied our bowlines to a sugar pine whose bark had been worn smooth by decades of boaters before us, and walked down to stare at the 15-foot vertical drop and the boiling

cauldron below. Standing at the lip of the falls, the spinning mist seemed to provide a perpetual rain on the banks and perhaps the reason for its name. Consulting the guidebook, I saw the etymology of the name, however, was less evocative. A nineteenth-century prospector and salmon gaffer named Reamy or Ramey was killed near the falls by Indians, and a bastardized version of his name was applied to the spectacle as a tribute.

Rainie Falls is rated VI on the international whitewater scale, meaning that there is a real risk of injury or even death. And even though it is usually run without mishap, Rainie has seen both. Running

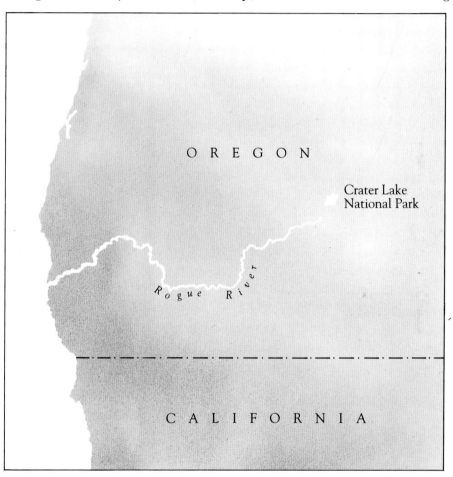

it would make spectacular footage, maybe the stuff that would put *Deliverance* in the archives. But it wasn't right for us, not that day. Not in a flimsy raft with three paddlers, including Joanne who had yet to hold her paddle correctly. Not even in the supercanoe, which although unsinkable had layers of fake birchbark coating that could be stripped off in big water.

So we portaged the heavy canoe around the left bank and relaunched it in the lapping water just below the falls. Then, after setting up Roger's camera on shore, the yellow raft made its way to the entrance of the fish ladder, a narrow staircase chute to the right of the falls that allows spawning salmon to travel upstream past Rainie and cautious rafters to make it downstream without portaging. The raft bounced down the chute like a pinball, and the camera pulled back to reveal Breck and me floating in the eddy below Rainie, as though we had just successfully negotiated the run. The magic of Hollywood.

We continued a long mile into the afternoon until we came to the broad beach at Whiskey Creek, where we made camp for the night. I set up my tent in a corner between a patch of yellow Siskiyou iris and fragrant wild azaleas and collapsed in exhaustion right after dinner.

We were on the river early the next day. The mist was still rising, doodling lazy curlicues in the cedars and hemlocks. An osprey wheeled above the fog; an otter splashed below. It was a glorious day.

We ran Tyee Rapids (*tyee* is the Chinook word for "chief"), practically shaving the grassy right bank, and at Wildcat we slalomed like Olympic skiers through a rock-garden course. By the time we got to Black Bar Falls, we had our river legs in the supercanoe and were feeling a bit cocky. So, when Roger gave the signal for action, we took off in a sprint, bolting over a series of six-foot drops, until we turned broadside, and a wave slapped the boat over, kicking Breck and me into the brink. In an instant the canoe popped back to its proper position sans crew.

"No, no," Roger screamed from shore.

We'd blown the shot. There was nothing in the script about a dual dunking and certainly no supercanoe that could right itself.

The next four days were long and scenic as we slowly made our way downstream, stopping at each rapid to set up the camera, a process that turned a two-minute run into two hours. But we didn't mind. We were far away from the battles being waged with the full production, a thought that didn't escape us when we floated by Battle Bar, the spot where more than 500 U.S. cavalry troops attacked 200 Rogue Indians, mostly women and children, during the bitter Indian wars of the 1850s.

On the morning of the last day, the river narrowed from its 100-foot width to a slim 15 feet as we slid into the two-mile-long Mule Creek Canyon. We bounced off the granite bedrock walls like billiard balls, caromed through the canyon into the Coffee Pot, an 8-foot passageway that has so many eddies that the river seems to be percolating. At a fern-draped tributary waterfall on the left bank, we emerged from the constricted chamber and knew there was just one rapid left—Blossom Bar, where the adventure began. Not long afterward we approached the rocks that had become so familiar a week before. The fear I had left behind resurfaced as we entered the run the hapless rafts had attempted. I knew the run by heart, with its demanding hard rights and lefts, and as we shoveled the water with our paddles, I stretched to see if the last wrapped raft was still there. I smiled. It wasn't. But the boulder was, and the water was tugging us toward it. I screamed at Breck to paddle harder. He screamed back at me to quit screaming. And we screeched around the boulder, glancing its tip with our stern, leaving behind a tiny stain of fake birchbark.

We were through. We paddled in quiet currents to our take-out at Foster Bar. Though we'd made it through Blossom Bar without broaching, it was, for us, at least in film patois, a wrap. And we paddled into the sunset, knowing that at least for a time, the Rogue, with its protected Wild and Scenic status, would not share the fate of our film production and its crew. When the cameras stopped rolling we would all go home, leaving nothing behind, taking with us the images, mental and celluloid. But the river would stay on and just keep rolling. For the Rogue, for now, there would be no wrap, and that seemed to me to be a happy ending.

The Rogue chisels through the bristled plateau of the Siskiyou Mountains.

Ed Cooper

99

James Thompson/Rapid Shooters

A run down the treacherous, boulder-choked right side of Blossom Bar. Named for the wild azaleas along its banks, Blossom Bar was so clogged with boulders that there was no passage until 1930. Then legendary riverman Glen Wooldridge blew the worst rocks out of the center of the river. But the right side of Blossom Bar remains a challenge for daring, or foolish, boaters.

James Thompson/Rapid Shooters

101

102

Rowing a self-bailing raft into the entrance of
Blossom Bar, the most technically difficult rapid
on the Rogue (above). The rapid is famous for
"wrapping" boats around the many boulders that dot
its football field–long obstacle course. Right: The
Rogue was one of the original eight rivers designated
as part of the Wild and Scenic Rivers System created in
1968, for reasons that are obvious here.

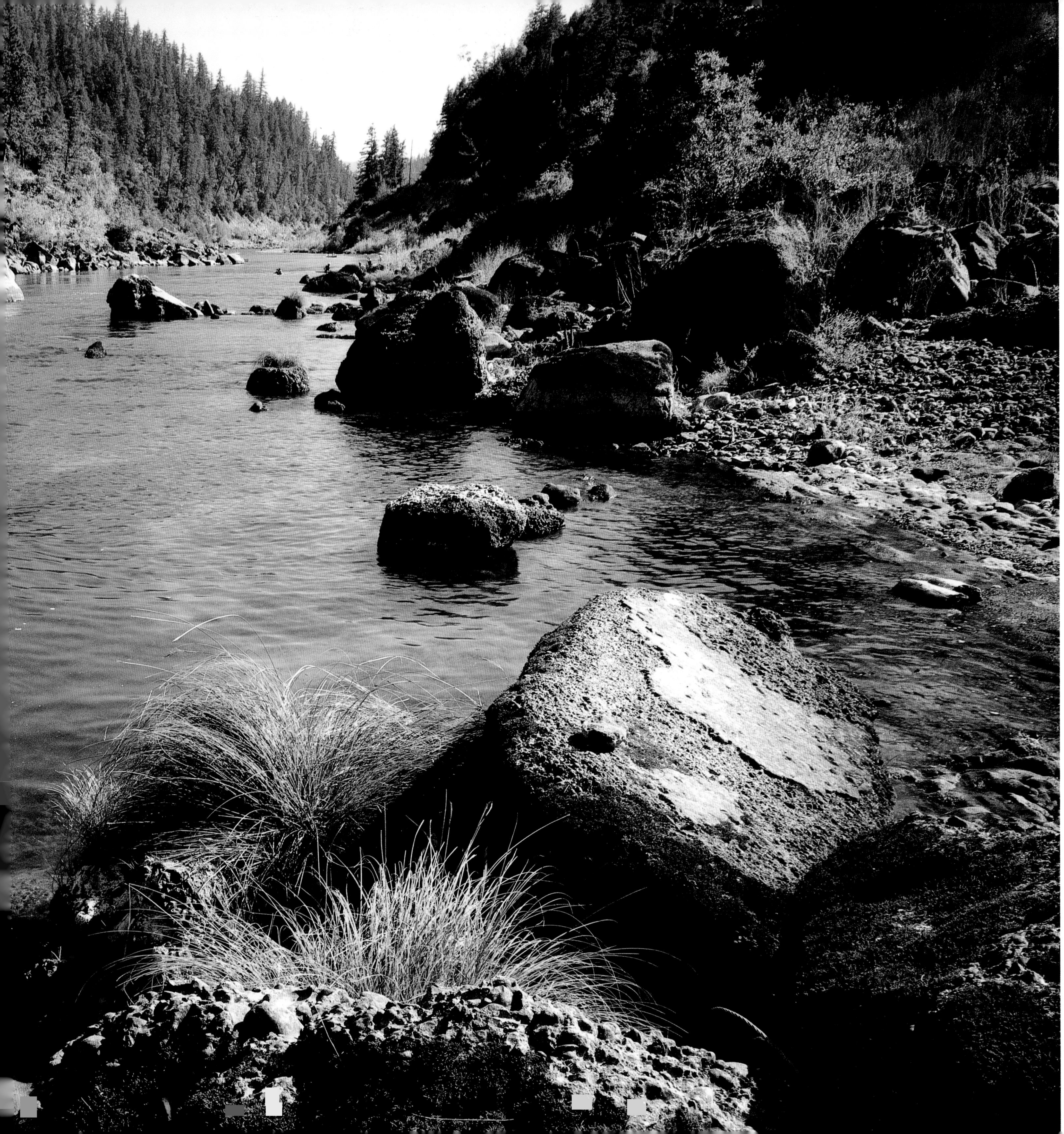

Ed Cooper

104

Bruce Dunn

The metavolcanic rocks of Hellgate Canyon, 13 miles above
the start of the wild section of the Rogue, house a deceptively
calm stretch of the scoundrel river, one available for recreational
boaters of intermediate skills.

Pistol Creek, Middle Fork of the Salmon River, Idaho.

SALMON

River of No Return

The word spread like wildfire. Tom Brokaw, the NBC newsman, had taken a trip down the Middle Fork of the Salmon with some friends. It was the end of June and the water was unusually high. Two of the three boats flipped in Weber Rapids, one of the last rapids. Brokaw made it to shore safely after a short swim in the 40-degree water. Two others weren't so lucky—Ellis Harmon, a 29-year-old Century City lawyer and militant Sierra Club member, and Gene Teague, 58, a long-time professional river guide who had been rowing at the moment of capsize. Four other people drowned that week on the Main and Middle forks of the Salmon.

Each had run a river of no return.

Almost a year after the drownings, I found myself with a couple of weeks off between Colorado River guiding assignments. I had read Brokaw's account of his trip in a magazine called *West* and was somehow drawn to the danger of the river. The Middle Fork was already a fabled whitewater run, and celebrity boaters such as Robert Kennedy, Arthur Godfrey, George Romney, and Jimmy Carter added luster to the legends. It was the wildest river in Idaho, and I knew I had to give it a try.

I had the time off, but two minor problems remained: I didn't have a car and I didn't have a raft. I recruited fellow Colorado River guide Breck O'Neill, and together we hitched to his mom's house in San Jose, where we convinced her to loan us her station wagon. We also picked up Breck's high school friends Dave Plapp and Mary Pollino, who, while not river runners, wanted to share in the adventure. Together we headed for central Idaho, the long way—in that we first went to Vernal, Utah (500 miles out of our way) and the warehouse of my employer, Hatch River Expeditions.

I cornered co-owner Don Hatch and asked if we could borrow a raft for our journey. Everyone knew that the river was Don's favorite; besides, his father, who had recently died, had made a pioneering run down the Middle Fork in 1936. So I thought we would be tugging at his heart strings with our appeal. Nonetheless, Don was not enthusiastic about loaning out one of the tools of his trade, especially to a young buck who the season before had ripped the bottom out of a company raft on the Colorado. I persisted, likening our quest to a holy mission, and at last he consented, warning us that we had to return the raft in exactly the same condition or we would have to pay for full replacement. He then pulled a black blob from the back of the warehouse, dusted off a layer of talcum powder, and presented us with our means of conveyance.

"She's one of my best boats. Take real good care of her." Don curled his lips.

I recognized that smile. It was on the face of a dealer who sold me a 1963 VW bug that blew up a week after I bought it. Still, we graciously accepted Don's offer, strapped the frame and oars on top of the station wagon, pushed the blob into the back, and waved good-bye.

The drive north into the massive western edge of the Rocky Mountains was humbling. To an easterner accustomed to the long rounded ridges of the Appalachians, these mountains seemed desolate and impenetrable. No wonder the Middle Fork and the Main Salmon had been spared dams, highways, and other modern developments, though not for lack of trying.

In 1805 William Clark, of the Lewis and Clark Expedition, attempted to explore the Salmon as a possible water route to the Columbia River, but he turned back when it became clear the rapids were impassable by boat and the canyon walls were too steep for horses and men. A century later, with the advent of specialized boats, access by water became a reality, but the rugged terrain still kept all but the most determined, and intrepid, at bay.

The following twilight we trundled into the Stanley Basin and at dusk arrived in Stanley, Idaho. We quickly found the hot spot in town— the thermal springs—and immediately slipped in for a soak. The night was so crisp the stars seemed to crackle and in the torpid curls of steam I could see the eddies and waves of the river we were about to encounter.

Designated by Congress in 1968 as part of the National Wild and Scenic River System, the Middle Fork of the Salmon is one of the last great American rivers remaining, throughout its course, unfettered by dams or hydro-projects of any kind. It begins life at the confluence of Bear Valley and Marsh creeks 20 miles northwest of the hot springs we

were enjoying. The source was discovered in 1863 by a mining party led by Captain John Stanley, for whom the closest town was named. Running in the shadows of the 2-mile-high peaks of the Sawtooth Range, the river plunges 1,600 feet in its 104-mile race to a union with the Main Salmon. Enroute it cascades through the Frank Church River of No Return Wilderness, renamed in 1984 after the late Idaho senator cited as one of America's "premiere wilderness champions."

At dawn the next morning we bounced down to the Dagger Falls put-in and, for the first time, unrolled our borrowed boat—a thin-skinned cotton neoprene survival raft shaped like an Easter basket. The raft was designed to carry a dozen survivors on the open sea with the sinking of the mother ship; it was not meant for sharp rocks or downriver negotiation. Yet, in a pinch, penny-pinching outfitters often used these boats, which could be purchased as government surplus, to carry clients on lenient runs. Our version looked as if it had already run the Styx—it was covered with patches and caramel streaks of hardened Barge glue.

"If this boat doesn't make it, we're all responsible for paying for a replacement," I reminded our little group as we all stared at the wad of rubber at our feet, a wad that looked more like a dead walrus than a raft.

Breck and Mary nodded in agreement. They were anxious to get on the river, whatever the costs or consequences. Dave took a couple of minutes before replying; he'd never been rafting and was questioning the wisdom of this little excursion.

But then he hesitatingly said, "Okay, I'm in," and we prepared ourselves to cast our fate to the river.

After repatching a half-dozen pinhole leaks, tying down the orange wooden frame, attaching the nine-foot white ash oars, we shoved off into the fast, cold currents of the Middle Fork and held on for a ride down a bolt of liquid lightning.

Almost immediately, before I had managed more than a dozen strokes, we whizzed by the first tributary on the left, Sulphur Creek, which thankfully was running below its banks. A year ago, another party had launched at Dagger Falls, a group of 19 led by Stanford University professor Don Wilson. A boat had flipped in the first minutes of the trip, leaving people on either side of Sulphur Creek, which was thundering into the Middle Fork in full spate. Wilson tied one end of a rope to a tree and the other to his waist and tried to swim the raging tributary to join those stranded on the other side.

One of the first rules of fast-river safety is never tie yourself to anything. If a rope goes taut, fluid mechanics takes over and forces any object at the end of the tethered line toward the river bottom, no matter the flotation. Don Wilson tried to swim across Sulphur Creek with the rope around his waist. In seconds he was swept downstream; the rope went taut. He was forced underwater like an anchor and drowned.

We had launched at an elevation of 5,700 feet and were dropping fast, some 42 feet per mile, on a water slide with no eddies, down a bowling alley with no gutters. I was at the oars, pulling frantically against the current to slow us down, but we were in the river's grip and were being pulled inexorably toward our first test: the coarse fabric of Velvet Falls.

The ranger at the Challis National Forest station had warned us about Velvet Falls, five miles below put-in, the first class IV rapid on the run. He said it had been and could be a killer, especially if run on the

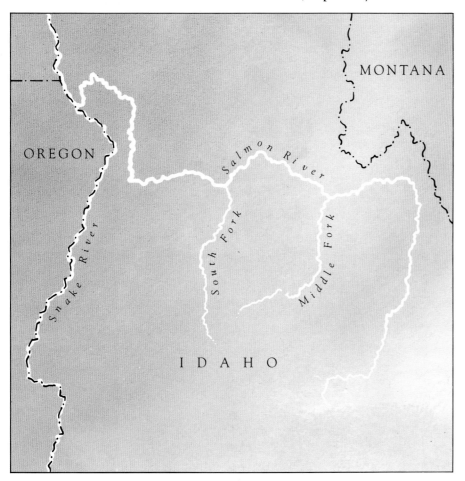

wrong side—the right—where it dropped sheer and spun a web of white-water chaos. The trick to running Velvet was to spot the large marker rock on the left while approaching and then position for a left-side plunge.

The advice seemed easy to heed, only now in the midst of the mill-race, I couldn't tell how fast we were going or how far we'd traveled.

"Think we've gone three miles yet?" I called out.

"I don't think so," Dave answered as we barreled down the right bank. Seconds later Breck screamed, "There's the marker rock. Pull over!" No way could I make the left shore, so I strained my back, pumped

the oars like pistons, and managed to scrape the eastern bank. Mary jumped out with the stern line and tried to hold us. But the boat wouldn't brake and she was dragged along the lichen-covered rocks, desperately grasping the end of the rope.

"It's burning," Mary's face wrenched in pain.

"Don't let go," Dave shouted back, but it was a useless call.

The rope yanked like a snapping winch cable from her raw hands, and the raft shot back into the current, heading for the lip of the deadly, right-hand side of Velvet Falls.

The three of us braced for the drop, and down we fell. The raft struck the bottom and started to twist sideways, as though crouching for a capsize. I took one concentrated, correcting stroke with the left oar, and *tang,* the oarlock snapped, sending the oar into orbit and me into the duffel pile. The raft kissed the edge of capsizing, then plopped back down and spun toward the right shore, where Breck was able to secure the boat to a tree.

The damage was minimal; the loop of the oarlock was gone, probably two dollars' worth of metal. But, it was a critical piece, and we had no replacement. So we found a sturdy piece of Engelmann spruce branch. I whittled it down to thoe-pin size with my Swiss army knife and then lashed the oar to the makeshift pin. The process took an hour, about the time it took Mary to thrash through the overgrowth to reach us. The jury-rigged oarpin setup didn't inspire confidence, especially since we had 34 rated rapids to go, but it was all we had. So, with my equanimity punctured, we reloaded and headed downstream.

The going was easier now, although rowing with an oarlock on one side and a crude thoe-pin lashed to the oar on the other made for less-than-smooth navigation. It was like running on crutches.

The next day we shot through Artillery and Cannon Creek rapids on target, not even a powder burn. We also passed tributaries named Mortar, Springfield, Winchester, Remington, Colt, and Popgun. The water was so cold it stung when it slapped my skin, and it was clearer than any I had ever seen. In the calm stretches I could lean over the raft and watch the colored, cobbled riverbed glide beneath me as though we were riding on glass. Sometimes the river was utterly still, the only movement the lazy turning of my own thoughts.

As though detonated, we blasted through the barrel-tight S-turn of Pistol Creek and then purled into Indian Creek, a level strip of bank where small planes bring in clients and gear during the later weeks of summer when the water is too low to launch upstream at Dagger Falls.

Though the river was fattening with each feeder stream, it didn't slow down, and for the next 30 miles we were treated to a full course of class II and III rapids, all in a setting that would rate VII on the I–VI

109

scale. Peaks surrounded us on all sides, the Salmon River Mountains to the west, the Bighorn Crags to the east, some craggy with bald rock faces, others blanketed with quilts of conifers and golden grasses. The canyon we were traversing was carved from the Idaho Batholith, a 100- by 200-mile mass of granite that once lay under volcanos long since eroded away, and dated at over 100 million years old.

On the third day, we came to Tappan Falls. Actually a series of four closely spaced drops, Tappan is rocky even in high water. The lashing holding the makeshift oarlock had loosened so that the blade of the oar bounced through the water as though rubber. I managed to steer the raft down the roiling right side of the river, but in the second drop the boat grated over a kernel of exposed granite, and the sound of the raft ripping drowned the rapids. In a flash Dave and Mary and the duffel pile were sucked out of sight, as though dropped through a trapdoor. I looked down between my legs and saw the river. The raft's bottom was gone, torn into two segments that flapped in the water like the wings of a stingray.

Frantically we wrestled the remains of our raft to shore, finally connecting at a small eddy below the last of the Tappan drops. Dave and Mary had splashed to shore a couple of hundred yards downstream and had made their way back up to our anchorage as Breck and I pulled the blob up onto a level spit of shore that was overrun with sharp grass, thornbushes, and ninebark. A bow-to-stern rip bisected the floor, a rip that would take at least a half day to repair. So, we gathered what had been retrieved of our gear, spread it out like pieces of a jigsaw puzzle to dry, and I set to work sewing the floor with a huge hooked needle and a spool of 30-pound-test nylon fishing line.

Clouds of mosquitoes rolled around our heads, and I spent more time scratching and slapping the air than patching. With the last rays of sunlight, I finished, pleased with my handiwork. I stepped onto one of the raft's tubes to raise my hand in triumph, and an explosion threw me to the ground. My weight had burst the tube. Half the boat was suddenly deflated, looking like a collapsed lung. While most inflatable whitewater rafts have at least four independent air chambers, and some have six, our little craft had just two. I looked closely; the fabric of the tube was rotten. The whole boat was cursed. Our expedition was coming apart at the seams. And we were halfway down the river, with the biggest rapids yet to go.

I suffered through a miserable night in my wet goosedown sleeping bag, listening to the river making obscene swallowing noises by our bivouac. With the first frosty light, I was up and patching. The repairs were finished by breakfast, but it took another half day for the glue to set. Dave, looking wan and feeble, had spent much of the night bent behind a tree. He was afflicted with giardiasis, picked up, we suspected, from the untreated Middle Fork water we'd all shared.

By noon we were on the water once again. We had only inflated the raft 80 percent to ease the pressure on its flimsy skin. We made it through Aparejo and then Haystack, where another boater had drowned the year before. At the confluence of Big Creek, we entered Impassable Canyon, where the worst of the Middle Fork rapids tore holes in the river. The gorge was named by U.S. First Cavalry Captain Reuben S. Bernard in 1879 when he led an ill-conceived expedition to capture the Sheepeater Indians in the area and was turned back by the terrain. Our expedition seemed equally ill-conceived. The river was now huge, the size of the Colorado, and a cold wind blew upstream as though from a tomb. We ran Porcupine Rapids with no new difficulties, then we careened through the center of Redside, a major rapid named for its colorful cutthroat trout.

Suddenly the floor I had so meticulously mended split open again, and once more the river yawned beneath me. I was out of control. My strokes meant nothing. And we were now in the angled waves of Weber Falls, the very rapid that had drowned Gene Teague and Ellis Harmon on Tom Brokaw's trip exactly a year before.

I struggled with the oars, threw my weight to the high side as we plunged through wave after giant wave, and saw my three companions doing the same, their faces white as the water. We dropped into a hole sideways, the frame cracked, and my tube patch blew out. Somehow we managed to hobble into the calm water below right-side-up, with everyone miraculously still in what was left of the boat.

Again we pulled over for repairs, but I had used all the Barge cement glue on the last round. Dave was slapping his sides, and his speech was slurred—the beginnings of hypothermia. We talked of hiking out, but the 4,000-foot-high walls were too steep. The gorge was named Impassable for a reason. With no interrupting edge of riverbank, the sheer flat rock face of dark gray granite formed a cryptlike chamber that revealed no end or exit. The map showed just 10 river miles to go and about as many rapids. We decided to go for it.

First, we relaid the patch that had popped off. Without new glue it barely stuck, so Mary agreed to sit on the patch, which reduced the situation to a slow leak. Then, we fastened the nozzle of the foot pump to the valve of the leaking tube with duct tape. Breck sat on the thwart with the foot pump in his lap and continued to pump with his hands as I rowed.

We limped through Cliffside, then with five miles left we rolled into Rubber. The waves were huge, as big as anything on the Colorado, and we rode them as though surfers on the North Shore. In the last wave the raft pitched up a crest, stalled at the top, and bent both bow and stern on opposite sides of the wave, and again we heard a horrifying *pop.* The other tube had split a seam, and half the raft immediately deflated. We all scrambled to a perch on the tube with the patch, and Breck continued to pump.

The frame hung limply, half in the water, completely useless. There was no way to row to shore. Dave threw me a terrified glance. All we could do was hang on. The blob with four passengers drooped through Hancock, Devil's Tooth, House Rocks, and Jump Off Rapids, and then we were finished. Like shipwreck survivors hanging onto flotsam, we drifted into the confluence, the clear water of the Middle Fork disappearing into the gray water of the Main.

When I returned the shredded blob of a boat to Don Hatch, I complained that it wasn't all it was cracked up to be. Don insisted it had been in perfect condition before we trashed it and held us to our end of the bargain—we had to pay for replacement. I swallowed and asked how much, thinking he'd want a thousand or more.

"Two hundred dollars and we'll call it even," he grinned that grin I recognized. Breck and Mary each handed in $50, but Dave said he was out of cash and asked if I'd cover him. I paid the final hundred and we went our separate ways.

I never heard from Dave Plapp again. He never sent a postcard, a letter, or a check. For a long time it bothered me that he never made good on his promise, although I really couldn't blame him since I was ultimately at fault. It was my trip, I had negotiated the use of the raft, and I was the oarsman. Now, through the gauzy lens of nostalgia I look back on that trip and smile. It was one of the most memorable, certainly one of the most exciting ever. So, Dave, if you read this, forget the $50—the Middle Fork experience was priceless.

Ted Weigold

112

*P*erhaps the su-
preme wilderness
*float trip, the Middle
Fork of the Salmon is
one of the last great
American rivers re-
maining, throughout
its course, unfettered
of dams or hydro-
projects of any kind.
Running in the shad-
ows of the 2-mile-
high peaks of the
Sawtooth Mountains,
the river plunges
1,600 feet in its 104-
mile rush to a union
with the Main
Salmon.*

Ted Weigold

Ted Weigold

114

Forty-miler stew tastes terrific even at Mile 51,
Pine Creek Flat, on the Middle Fork. The river
cascades through the 2,361,767-acre Frank Church
River of No Return Wilderness, named after the late
Idaho senator cited as one of America's "premiere
wilderness champions."

116

Ted Weigold

Isolated and remote, the Middle Fork nestles in the heart of the Salmon River Mountains, a chaotic jumble of peaks and ridges north of the tumultuous crags of the Sawtooth Mountains. So formidable are the approaches that pioneers long avoided the canyon of the Middle Fork. Yet this isolation, and a series of 40 world-class rapids, spectacular fishing, soothing hot springs, and magnificent camping, now make the river corridor a magnet for river runners.

117

Pat O'Hara

The Snake River as it winds past the Teton Range, Wyoming.

Ed Riddell

SNAKE

In the Shadow of the Tetons

Rising from southeastern Yellowstone National Park in Teton County, northwest Wyoming, the Snake begins like a gnome getting up in the morning, a tiny rascal that spins and dances and digests until 1,038 miles later it collapses, fat and exhausted, into the arms of the Columbia.

When French-Canadian explorers reached the middle Snake in 1811, they called it *la maudite rivière enragée* ("the accursed mad river"). When Breck O'Neill arrived in the broad valley of Jackson Hole in 1976, he decided to name his floating company Mad River. And, when I arrived in the spring of 1980 to help Breck on a project on the Snake, I just went mad.

It was a Hollywood discovery story straight from the streets of Tinseltown to the banks of the Snake. Mike Sammons—33, bald, shy, and about as rugged as baby booties—was feeling lucky just to have the $4-an-hour job driving the film-crew bus from a Jackson Hole hotel to a location along the upper Snake. He had no idea what serpentine fate awaited him.

The 60-person crew was in town filming *Pursuit of D. B. Cooper*, a $15-million chase movie based loosely on the escapades of the mysterious and imaginative extortionist who jumped out of a Northwest Orient 727 airliner in 1971 with $250,000 in cash.

Casablanca Filmworks (*Midnight Express* and *The Deep*) and its parent company, Polygram, were producing the film, due for release the following summer. Somehow director John Frankenheimer (*Manchurian Candidate*, *Birdman of Al-*

catraz) had decided that the film's pivotal sequence was to be a whitewater chase between a Federal Aviation Administration investigator (played by Robert Duvall) in a 13-foot Avon inflatable raft and D. B. Cooper (played by Treat Williams) in a wooden dory. In Frankenheimer's words, the scene would be the grand prix of river running, the ultimate whitewater film footage.

The Snake, to me, has always evoked the image of wilderness at its most spectacular—a pristine landscape, a cold, clean, limpid river. The Snake River valley seemed a place to go on retreat, a spot to escape the complexities and pressures of city life, a simple, innocent river that slaked the thirst of the Nez Percé, mountain men, and rafters. I had always wanted to float its twisting course, but had never imagined the opportunity would come in the form of a major Hollywood production. Now, standing on the Snake's high sagebrush-covered banks, with a flurry of snowflakes dusting the tops of the aspens, I was watching the ultrasophisticated, elaborate, calculated movements of a multimillion-dollar movie machine, and it all seemed out of place and time.

The Snake River through Jackson Hole was chosen as the principal locale for shooting the "ultimate whitewater" because Paul Sylbert, the art director, had a passion for fly fishing and had heard the Snake offered some of the best in the country. The job of bringing the whitewater sequences together fell to Breck O'Neill, my old friend and former Colorado River guide, and his company, Mad River Boat Trips. Sylbert picked the company from a guidebook because he liked the name.

Two years earlier, Breck had been co-owner of a rafting company that operated through the Hualapai Indian Reservation in the Lower Grand Canyon, when he found himself in a dispute with the Indians who sanctioned his concern. They gave him until sundown to get out of town. He loaded up his truck and headed north. Breck landed on the banks of the Snake, the river he had heard was the most popular rafting river in the world, with over 100,000 people floating its spangled waters each summer. He figured there would be room for him.

Now, with the prospect of a major motion picture on his doorstep, Breck asked me if I would come and help. I hopped the first plane and flew into Jackson Hole with the glistening band of the Snake summoning and the 13,770-foot-high Grand Teton Peak watching with regal approval.

Fifty miles from Jackson, just before the Snake swings northwest and crosses into Idaho, the Greys, a major tributary, tumbles from the Tetons. For its last 15 miles, it falls 50 feet a mile and during June flood, it runs about 3,000 cubic feet per second. Never before run by raft or dory, the Greys was full of boulder-strewn technical rapids. It gave Breck the wild whitewater he was hired to find.

My job was to help Breck stage the whitewater sequences, but when the director saw me, he asked if I'd like to be Robert Duvall's double. I looked in the mirror and couldn't see the resemblance, aside from a receding hairline. But I agreed, and within hours my hair was being cut by a Hollywood stylist flown in just to make me look the part. The barber told me that including his airfare, the total cost for my haircut was $500, a figure that exceeded the grand total I had spent on my hair to that point in my life.

Finally, with my forehead sheared in Duvallesque fashion, I was escorted to the front of the raft I would be riding. Breck would row, playing the guide for Duvall's character, and I would cower in the bow as we crashed through the rapids. The director told me to act like a terrified rookie while the cameras were running, and I nodded, thinking that would be easy. On the first run, the boat was tossed like a bubble on a breeze and I tried to act like the Robert Duvall I remembered from *The Godfather* and *Apocalypse Now*. But Frankenheimer didn't like my acting, my face, my haircut, and especially my body movements. He screamed at me to look away from the cameras. As we plunged through waves and into holes, I instinctively threw my weight to the high side to prevent capsizing, which is the opposite of what an amateur would do. On the second run, he dressed me in a poncho with the hood up and drawn tight. He coached me. I had to look frightened, unfamiliar, awkward. We tried again, but it was still no go. I looked too seasoned in the rapids, and the script called for raw terror.

Then someone happened to notice the bus driver, Mike Sammons. As fate would have it, soft-spoken, timid Mike was a Robert Duvall clone. Never mind that he had never shot a rapid in his life, had never even camped out, or that he lived with his mother, who at 63 years old was the family breadwinner. He was a casting dream come true.

"Mike, for five hundred dollars a day would you run these rapids? All you have to do is hang on while Breck rows. Trust us," Frankenheimer implored.

John Frankenheimer is a director who gets his way, and a half hour later Mike was dressed as I had been, only without the hood, and barreling down the river. He was perfect. Not only did he look like Robert Duvall, he looked terrified. His white knuckles spat light like beacons and at the end of his first run, I pulled in the raft and saw frays on the gunwale rope he had been gripping.

For the first days Mike did beautifully as the Duvall double, acting naturally and making more money than he would in a year of bus driving. He handled it all with quiet but wide-eyed aplomb as he was dumped into giant souse holes and hydraulics the likes of which most professional river guides wouldn't touch. But Frankenheimer kept pushing for more action, and Breck, at the oars, tried to accommodate. At one point Mike was washed from the boat, swept under a tree snag, bounced, bruised, and nearly drowned. But he kept going, and he kept earning more money.

"How about an extra hundred if you run that rapid again?" Frankenheimer would ask with his arm around Mike's shoulder.

"Sure, I guess so," Mike would shrug.

Those of us watching from shore kept wondering if the guy was brave, stupid, or just greedy. In the meantime, I felt like a fifth wheel. Once I wandered off and came on a moose posing by a quiet stretch of river. It was a scene in the script, so I ran to the nearest grip, borrowed his

walkie-talkie, and tuned into Frankenheimer's frequency.

"John, we've got the scene with the moose right here. It's perfect. If you hurry, I'm sure you can get it."

"Thanks, but we don't need any real animals. We'll get that back at the studio. Where's Mike? We need another take."

On day six, trouble struck—but not on the river. Bill Tennant, the producer, joined the set and decided he didn't like Mike, nonunion and nonprofessional, doing hairy stunt work meant for Hollywood experts. So he called in Dean Ferrandini, professional Hollywood whitewater stuntman. Ferrandini showed up with a capped-tooth smile and a $50

haircut, a tenth the cost of mine and looking 10 times better. He bypassed the team of kayakers who had been coordinating the rescue/safety procedures, the doubles who had been running the rapids, and me, the newly appointed whitewater technical adviser. He went straight to Frankenheimer and started talking stunts with cables, wires, and quick releases attached to rafts at precisely measured locations so that the boats would stand on end, tip, contort, and act like puppets on cue.

It sounded phony to me and to most of the crew, but Frankenheimer listened and gave him the green light. Ferrandini also asked that a team of stunt friends be flown in immediately from Los Angeles to replace Breck, Mike, and the other doubles.

The next day the shooting moved to Lunch Counter Rapid on the Snake, the one piece of significant turbulence on the standard, commercial, 20-mile run between Pacific Creek Landing and Moose. Sliding like speeding syrup into a gray granite wedge, the river reared back and kicked its frosty-white feet like a stubborn old mule.

As the cameras were being positioned, two sets of Duvall doubles lined the banks. Breck, who had been promised the part of the river guide, saw Frankenheimer hand Ferrandini the guide's script. Breck knew he was in danger of losing a job and so did Mike. Just before the first take of the run through Lunch Counter, Breck and Mike put their heads together.

"Listen, Mike, if you like this job, if you like the money, you've got to do something really spectacular in this run. You've got to fall out of the boat in the biggest wave. You've got to swim this rapid."

"But I can't do that."

"Why not?"

"I can't swim."

At the call for action, Breck pulled the oars and maneuvered the tiny raft into the current. Seconds later, the raft dropped into the first trough, slammed into a wall of water, stopped dead for a fraction of a second, shimmied, and rode over the top of a wave—just as Mike disappeared from the boat. Breck dropped the oars in horror, leaped to the bow, clutched at Mike, grabbing the back of his poncho and pulling him back in as the river spread into a placid sheet.

The filmmakers cheered from the shore. It was a sensational shot, one that Ferrandini's "professional stunt team" had been planning, but never got the chance to perform.

"I'll give you an extra two-fifty to do that again, Mike," Frankenheimer beamed while pumping Mike's hand.

"Okay, I guess so . . ."

That put Ferrandini and his team out of work for the rest of the day. The following morning, as a band of clouds gathered over the sun,

121

Frankenheimer agreed to let Ferrandini attempt to execute some "technical" stunts. The first one was a rig with cables running from both sides of the riverbank to the raft, measured so that when the boat fell into a small hole 10 yards downstream, it would appear to be stuck in recirculating water. Four times Ferrandini tried and four times it looked like a raft attached to cables. At $140,000 a day in shooting costs, Frankenheimer was losing patience.

After lunch, Ferrandini had another stunt concocted. This time, dressed as D. B. Cooper, he would row the dory through a rock-laced rapid and hit a certain lodgepole pine log halfway down the stretch, get stuck, then push the boat back into the current, finally just missing a mammoth undercut log stretched halfway across the rushing river. This log, set as it was in the midst of strong river currents, was a potential death trap, a configuration all too common to river fatalities. For this projected run, Ferrandini was putting one of his stunt people, Paula, in the bow of the dory as Cooper's wife. Paula was brave, but she had little river experience. It was a risky proposition of seemingly little celluloid value, but he got the go-ahead and pushed off as the crew on shore held its breath.

The run started spectacularly enough when an oar came loose from its clip and spun the boat out of control. Unfortunately, the dory went nowhere near the plotted course, was out of camera sight almost throughout, and hit a rock that punched a fist-sized hole in the hull. But it came out right-side-up, riders safe and intact.

"Get that Ferrandini on the champagne flight back to L.A.," Frankenheimer squawked over his walkie-talkie.

Each night after that incident, we would assemble at the nearby racquet club for showings of the previous day's footage. The film was jetted to Los Angeles for developing, then flown back to our private viewing room on the shores of the Snake. On the ninth night Frankenheimer announced he had all the footage he needed, except for one shot. In the script, as the two boats exited Jackson Lake at the start of the chase, they plummeted over a waterfall. He needed a spectacular, breathtaking waterfall to stage the scene.

So, the next morning under gunmetal skies, we drove up the Snake River Road somber as members of a funeral procession, stopping at a tiny tributary of the Snake, aptly named Fall Creek, that flowed as clear as mountain air. Just 200 yards above its confluence with the Snake, the stream dropped over an 18-foot ledge into a boiling pool. No raft or dory had ever been near these falls.

"It's a piece of cake, Mike," Breck offered unconvincingly. Mike said nothing that morning until he walked to the lip of the falls and looked down.

"That's no piece of cake," he said, shaking his head.

"Tell you what, Mike," Frankenheimer coaxed. "I'll pay you a base of a thousand for this shot, plus two-fifty each time you go over the falls. Whadda ya say, buddy?"

The tension was thick enough to slice as the Avon Adventurer raft bobbed toward the precipice of the falls. Mike crouched in the bow, white-knuckled fingers holding tight. Then, as the boat pitched over the edge, a blood-curdling scream pierced the roar of the water. It was a scream totally out of control, involuntary, and so high-pitched I thought it must have come from a woman. But it was Mike. The boat hit bottom, buried in a confusion of water and spray, then bounced up and out, the boat and Mike unpunctured, unscathed. As the crew ushered a wobbly-legged Mike to shore, the camera crew thundered applause. Someone shoved a walkie-talkie in his face, and Frankenheimer's voice crackled praise from across the creek.

Minutes later Mike was above the falls in the boat for another take. This was an establishing shot, he was told, the boat would float just to the edge of the falls; it would not go over. But, seconds before rolling, Frankenheimer changed his mind and decided he wanted another run over the falls. Nobody bothered to tell Mike. So, as the raft launched and sailed downstream toward the abyss, Mike was none the wiser.

This time he didn't even scream. Those of us watching believe he never realized he made the second plunge until he received his check. But, again, he and the boat bounced from the base of the falls in good shape. Frankenheimer was heady with success and entreated Mike for one more try. A glassy-eyed nod from Mike, and within the hour he was airborne once more, emerging from the bottom $1,750 richer for his day's efforts (though his total time spent in the raft was clocked at 12 minutes).

As the cameras, battery-packs, and tripods were being packed into the studio semis, Frankenheimer sauntered over to Mike and bestowed his commendations, offering to get him into the Screen Actors Guild and to help him carve out a new career as Robert Duvall's double.

"What'll you do with all the money you've earned?" the famous Hollywood director asked the Jackson Hole bus driver.

"Ahhh . . . I think I'll buy my mother a gift and take her on vacation. And maybe now she can retire from housekeeping."

Nobody on the set deserved the mad money more. As the Frontier Airlines prop plane took off for points south carrying the largest Hollywood contingent ever to invade the little river community, Jackson Hole settled back into its summer tourism routine, a million dollars richer and with a new motto: Life, Liberty, and the Happiness of the Pursuit of D. B. Cooper.

122

123

Aspens at the Oxbow Bend of the Snake River in Grand Teton National Park, Wyoming.

Larry Ulrich

124

Barker Ewing

Lunch Counter Rapid on the Snake, the largest rapid of the 20-mile run between Pacific Creek Landing and Moose, Wyoming. Sliding like speeding syrup into a gray-granite wedge, the river rears back and kicks out like a mule.

Pat O'Hara

The moose is the largest living deer in the Northern Hemisphere with antlers that sometimes spread six feet across (above). Several hundred moose graze the Snake River banks, enjoying the roughage of evergreen bark and the succulence of water plants. Right: The Snake flows gently through Grand Teton National Park at sunrise.

127

128

Ed Riddell

Jeff Foott

129

When French-Canadian explorers reached the middle Snake in 1811, they called it la maudite rivière enragée ("the accursed mad river"), and today it continues to live up to that description with rapids that blur with rage.

The Tatshenshini River, Alaska–British Columbia, Canada.

TATSHENSHINI

Out of the Yukon

t was another sweltering, stinky July afternoon in Los Angeles. The radio droned a second-level smog alert. I was cloistered in my bedroom putting the finishing touches on my master's thesis—a futile project, since for every typo I corrected, a bead of sweat leaped off my forehead onto the paper like grease popping from a pan. Finally, my last eraser broke and I staggered to the kitchen to stick my head in the refrigerator.

"God, I'd rather be anywhere than here," I mumbled, wrenching open the door to a half-eaten, half-melted baked Alaska. The fridge had stopped. I imagined hurling myself out of my first-floor window, clutching an empty ice tray in lieu of a suicide note, when the phone across the room started to vibrate. Seconds later, after traveling through an atmosphere as thick as glue, the ringing reached my ears.

It was my old rafting friend, Bart Henderson. He was organizing a rafting expedition to Alaska and wanted to know if I would join. The call was like manna from heaven.

That night I tried to imagine what I'd just committed myself to. Alaska! All I knew about the forty-ninth state were the pieces of popular culture that drift into everyone's consciousness: Eskimos rubbing noses; totem poles; Mount McKinley; cold; Nanook; glaciers; cold; black flies; mosquitoes; grizzlies; severe cold. The river appeared in my mind's eye: a whitewater torrent slicing through barren tundra, cloaked in a mantle of mosquitoes and biting flies, bordered by savage grizzlies, filled with serrated ice floes, and enveloped in a perpetual blizzard.

Still, it was better than L.A.

The next week was spent in hurried preparation for something I really didn't know how to prepare for. I did some research and found that few generalizations can be applied to a land as vast and varied as Alaska, a state twice the size of Texas. In the midst of summer, when the days are 18 hours or longer, there's little time for cooling and temperatures in the 90s are common. In fact, according to the U.S. Weather Bureau, the highest recorded temperature in Anchorage is 100° F, while the highest in Miami Beach is only 98°?

I found that our target river, the Tatshenshini, springs forth in the Yukon, flows southwest through British Columbia and into Alaska's panhandle. It empties its turbid load into Dry Bay in the Tongass National Forest, just above Glacier Bay National Park. It sounded cold, yet August was the state's hottest month.

So, I gathered up my long underwear and my cutoffs, my down vest and my Solarcaine®. I bought a mosquito-net hat, a pair of wet-suit booties, a new poncho, and a pair of polarized sunglasses. And I was off to expedition headquarters (Bart's driveway). Bart had billed our upcoming exercise as "the river trip of the century" and had invited Sir Edmund Hillary, Lowell Thomas, Jacques Cousteau, David Brower, and other wilderness-adventure luminaries. Instead he got 10 part-time river guides, including a beach bum, a couple of carpenters, a truck driver, a gas station owner, and me, a frustrated graduate student.

Our lack of notoriety notwithstanding, we were a tight-knit, highly capable group well versed in the ways of the wilderness. The only trouble was that five of us had neglected to bring tents, three had no rain gear, and the maps had been misplaced. After a visit to a sporting goods store, where we also purchased one of the rafts we would need to run the Tat (as it was immediately nicknamed), we piled into our cars and headed north.

At Prince Rupert in British Columbia, we boarded the Alaska Ferry and started sailing up the Inside Passage toward Haines, which is north of Juneau. From there we would drive the final hundred miles or so to the put-in at an abandoned fishing camp called Dalton Post.

Haines, the northern terminus of the Alaska Marine Highway, is majestically backdropped by the Cathedral Peaks of the Chilkat Mountains and its waterfront faces the Chilkoot Inlet of the Lynn Canal, an 80-mile-long fjord. The town is an Arcadian outpost with a population of about a thousand and one library rich in the lore of the region. It was here I first found information on the Tatshenshini.

Although it finally carries more water than the Colorado, the Tat is a tributary to the larger Alsek. In fact, the last 50 miles of our trip would be on the Alsek. Both rivers knife through the ridiculously rugged St. Elias Range, which counts among its prizes Mount Logan, Canada's

highest at 19,524 feet, and Mount St. Elias at 18,008 feet. Forming a base for this array of peaks is an ice-covered plateau known as the Icefield Ranges. Dating back to the last ice age, these massive fields of snow and ice are maintained by the moist Pacific air flowing over the mountains.

According to the Alaska Geographic Society, the first exploration of the Tatshenshini by white men, from near its source to its junction with the Alsek and on to the sea, was in 1890. Edward James Glave led a party of six men up the Chilkat River and overland to Kusawa Lake. Four of them continued to the Yukon while Glave and Jack Dalton, the packer and guide who later established the Dalton Trail into the interior, went down the Tatshenshini. Glave wrote several articles in a popular New York weekly about the hair-raising trip, dismissing the route as unfeasible.

If prospectors headed for the Klondike during the 1898 gold rush ever read the series, they must have discounted it as newspaper sensationalism. The Alsek–Tatshenshini route still looked like a way inland and over 300 prospectors tried it. Only 12 survived.

The first descent of the Alsek from Haines Junction to Dry Bay may have been made in 1961 by Clem Rawert and John Dawson, though some of the gold rush prospectors did impossible things that were never recorded.

D. B. Crouch, who went down the Alsek in March 1970, called his expedition "the second descent" when his account appeared in the March 1971 issue of *Alaska* magazine. Because of surges in the Tweedsmuir Glacier, which impelled the giant river (50,000 cubic feet per second) up against the opposite wall, creating a nine-mile stretch of pure whitewater hell, Crouch and his party of three were stopped halfway down the river. It was impossible to portage across, and Crouch concluded that the canyon was unrunnable.

The Tatshenshini, however, looked to be a different matter. In early September 1972, Richard Norgaard and three friends made the 150-mile float in seven days from Dalton Post to the inappropriately named Dry Bay on the Gulf of Alaska. Still another party, led by Bill Kenyon of Glennallen, Alaska, made the river trek. Each group described the Tatshenshini as an exceptionally beautiful whitewater wilderness trip.

In Haines, I also contracted "bearanoia." The town seemed to be preoccupied with the animal. The one theater was playing the film *Grizzly* (honest), held over since December. Several stores sold a device billed as "Grizz Repellent," consisting of a simple slow-paced strobe light. It came with a money-back guarantee, which made good marketing sense, since if it didn't work, it was unlikely the purchaser would make it back for a refund.

After picking up the last of the needed supplies and registering with the Haines magistrate, in case we didn't come back, we were off for Dalton Post, the river starting point. The drive north lifted us over the Coastal Range out of the rain forest, and for the first time in days we were splashed with sunshine and blue sky. The transition was akin to Dorothy's passage from black-and-white Kansas to a multicolored Oz.

Crossing into the Yukon, Canadian Customs sealed our .357 MAGNUM® pistol in a plastic bag, not to be opened for the duration of our stay in Canada. (Handguns are illegal in Canada.)

"But officer, what'll we do if a grizzly attacks?"

"Throw the gun at him. If you open that bag, you'll wish a grizzly had gotten you before the Royal Canadian Mounted Police."

We meandered over a sparsely vegetated plateau at 6,000 feet and then wound down into the green river valley of the Tatshenshini. It took some looking and retracing and wheel spinning to find the right dirt road down to the put-in. The road was marked by a sign that read in bright, bold letters: *Public Notice: The public is warned that grizzly bears are abundant in this area and must be considered dangerous.*

Mounties or no, we ripped the plastic off the .357 and headed down to the river.

The Tat was milky and fast, probably dashing by at five miles per hour. The water temperature measured 47° F, which didn't seem all that cold, considering. Just downstream, the Klukshu River, a diamond-clear tributary, entered the Tat. The Klukshu was choked with chinook (king) and sockeye salmon, so thick you could shovel them to shore.

We were at 2,000-feet elevation on a beach that hoary marmots darted across like mechanical targets. All around us was a primeval world of bristly Sitka spruce, western hemlock, and quaking poplar and alder. On a nearby branch a whisky jay eyed us vapidly. And in the background stood the saw-toothed, snow-salted beginnings of the St. Elias Range.

Suddenly a frantic yelp broke our reverie.

"Oh my God, look at this!"

We scrambled over to a practically cataleptic Doug, who was standing with both his boots inside the footprint of a grizzly. The tracks crossed the beach and disappeared into the river.

Without wasting much time, we swung into action. Bart built a platform in the trees to store our food for the night. The rest of us started to drink lots of water. (I'd read somewhere that the one way to keep grizzlies at bay was to urinate around camp. The bears use urine to mark their own territory and it's a boundary they respect.)

We all awoke intact the next morning—Friday the thirteenth—the lucky launching day. Outside the tent were unfamiliar voices—two fellows with the Canadian Fish and Game Department who were working up the Klukshu River counting salmon. They told us that earlier that summer two kayakers had twice tried to make it down the Tatshenshini, but both times had been thwarted when their boats were destroyed in a gorge an hour downstream. They had to hike out.

As if trying to dampen an otherwise nice day, our visitors then pointed out that while it was sunny and warm at the moment, the weather was particularly volatile, and the temperature might drop below zero in a matter of hours. A year ago that day, they claimed, seven inches of snow had covered where we were now standing.

At 4:00 we broke a bottle of tonic water (in lieu of champagne) on an oar and shoved off. A vital force took hold of us; the banks zipped by almost too fast to register. I felt the complicated urgency of the current. A brisk wind slapped my face. At a boulder a few hundred yards downriver, we all caught an eddy and celebrated with a slug of Yukon Jack.

That evening we camped only two miles from our starting point at the pebbled mouth of Village Creek, which once flowed through a small Chinook Indian village. We were all a little ruffled about the rumored gorge that ate up kayaks, so we decided to wait and tackle it the next day. We might need the extra daylight if there were indeed bad stretches requiring extensive scouting or portaging.

The camp beach was littered with grizzly tracks, so once again we drank up and cordoned the area, a ritual repeated throughout the trip. The evening was almost balmy. A bowl of chili, a cup of coffee, and a peaceful night on the Tatshenshini.

Bang! My head exploded in shock. I was in a shaking cave filled with cold steam. I was in the water, icy water, and I knew a body could function for only a matter of minutes in water this cold. Death follows quickly. I had to get to the boat fast. My arms dug into the crashing water, water that pricked at my skin like a thousand ice picks. Suddenly, I was at the bow. I reached up, grabbed the gunwale painter, and tried to pull myself in. I couldn't. I was losing strength. Then, Stan appeared over the bow. He clutched my life jacket and somehow pulled my blue-skinned body in. We were in the gorge.

We had arrived an hour after camp and found a sporting stretch of whitewater, or graywater as it should be called with its high granitic silt concentrations. With Stan at the oars, we were suddenly sucked sideways into a chalky hydraulic, a trough of recirculating water. The boat stopped dead, then shimmied violently, pitched and canted to one side, dumping me into the churning currents. Six eternal seconds later I was back in the boat. In three more seconds the boat was free of the hydraulic, and I was frantically bailing. Stan grappled the boat to shore so I could change clothes, and Dick, in his kayak, made a comedic capsize trying to pull up next to us. The river had proved its power.

133

The gorge lasted for four exciting, exhausting miles, then gave way to steep valley. Overhead two bald eagles soared in splendorous flight, the first of dozens we would see. The area we were floating through hosts one of the greatest concentrations of bald eagles in the world.

With two of us damp from dunkings, we pulled over early to camp at the mouth of a gushing tributary called Silver Creek. After a sauna rigged from ground cloths, ponchos, and crossed oars, we retreated into a long sleep.

Clack, clack, clang echoed through the still forest. We had been warned that it was unsafe to hike in this area without a bell or noisemaker to scare away grizzlies. We had searched Haines and could only come up with a single dinner bell and no clapper. So, now that Skip, Tim, and Doug were going fishing up Silver Creek they jury-rigged noisemakers— Sierra Club cups and Swiss army knives hanging from their belts. Then, off they went into the fog.

I wandered the periphery of the camp through rags of mist for an hour and found four sets of moose antler and scores of cloven tracks. The Alaskan moose tips the scales at up to 1,800 pounds, and each antler can weigh up to 85 pounds.

Then, like thunderclaps, the whole universe reverberated with two closely spaced booms. It was Skip's Winchester. Either a grizzly had confronted him and it was too late to retreat, or he was firing at a moose or some game animal. The shots were too close together for target practice.

We paced the fire, speculating. If Skip didn't show in a half hour, we'd form a search party and head up the creek. Twenty-five minutes later, an enormous grin appeared out of the thicket. Behind it was Skip shouldering a 25-pound chinook salmon on a stick. That fish was cleaned and cut into fat steaks in no time. We fanned the fire to get some good coals and minutes later were feasting on the silky smooth meat of salmon fresher than any restaurant could ever offer.

An hour later we were back on the pewter-colored river, and according to our maps we passed from the Yukon into British Columbia, although there was nothing tangible to prove this.

Then we saw him: Old Ephraim, Gyas, Grizz, *Ursus arctos horribilis*, the fiercest animal in the Northwest—the grizzly bear. As fast as a horse for short distances and stronger than a dozen men, the grizzly is one of the few animals in the world that will attack a human unprovoked.

He was poised on the right bank. Once the word was passed of his presence, there was nothing but hypnotic silence. He presented an elegant sight. As we drifted closer, he looked up in dispassionate curiosity. Then, without a hint of fear, he moped off into the thicket. But before he vanished, Bart pointed to the opposite shore. There, directly across, was another grizzly. As we pulled cameras from waterproof boxes, Dick

started to kayak toward the second grizzly. There were some muffled objections. Grizzlies are not only fast on land, they're good swimmers.

If you needed to escape from one, you could try climbing a tree. Grizzlies can't climb as well as their smaller cousin, the black bear, because they don't have retractable claws. But they do get to be about eight feet tall, and when you add in however long their legs are, they probably could reach a hell of a long way up that tree. Plus with their tough skin and thick skull and forehead plate, it is very difficult to kill a grizzly with a single shot of almost any gun—and often there's time for just one shot.

So Dick cautiously paddled over toward the burly animal, while we covered him from the raft. The chances were good that this grizzly had never seen or smelled humans before. Dick braced and held about 20 feet from shore. The grizzly's head was tilted in wonderment. He was a young bear, less than 500 pounds. (Full-grown adults can exceed 1,000 pounds.) He certainly didn't know the meaning of fear. We certainly did.

Dick spoke to the bear as though coaxing a dog to let him near the mailbox. Grizz responded with wide eyes and flared nostrils. He didn't know what to make of the aquatic intruder. A 15-minute interlude ensued during which Grizz followed on shore as Dick drifted downstream. It wasn't a malicious pursuit, rather one of curiosity. The game ended abruptly with a cliff that prevented the bear from following us downstream. With a glance of what seemed to be regret, he turned and ambled off into the alders.

That night we made sure we camped on an island. We figured we would at least have some warning if a bear tried to splash across the strong current in the middle of the night. But next morning the beach was crisscrossed with fresh pizza-sized tracks, and nobody had heard a sound.

Breakfast was cornmeal mush, granola, oranges, and crisp Canadian air. We floated through a natural aviary, passing semipalmated plovers, spotted sandpipers, northern phalaropes, water pipits, pine siskins, tree swallows, willow ptarmigans (clumsy game birds), a variety of hawks and falcons, honking Canada geese, and others.

At noon, we swung by the base of the Alsek Range, which separated us from the Alsek River basin by 8,000 feet and 50 miles. Here the river turned south and ran adjacent to the mountains for 50 miles before cutting directly into them. Here also we saw glaciers for the first time— brilliant blue rivers of ice bisecting spires and summits, oozing toward the center of the earth.

We camped that night in a bed of wispy white wildflowers near a sediment-filled creek, surrounded by scores of cascading waterfalls, some several hundred feet high. In the Southwest, any one of these waterfalls would be a major tourist attraction. But here they're so numerous that we soon stopped paying attention to them.

The fourth morning we woke to a delicate frost sprinkled across the flowers, and a heavy smoke of fog that moved just a little slower than the current, rolling down the water in huge billows. Downstream, after the sun stretched and yawned and warmed things up to a toasty 75 degrees, Dick offered to let others try his kayak (his was the only kayak on the trip; the rest of us were divided among the three rafts).

Kal, an absolute beginner but strong on enthusiasm, quickly volunteered. He climbed into the kayak just when the river twisted into an oxbow that was crammed with logs and snags, the bane of boatmen.

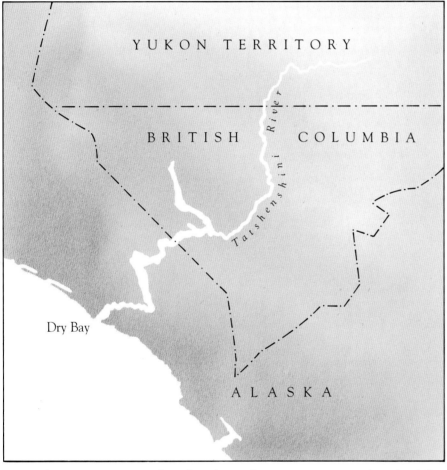

More drownings occur when kayaks and canoes get pinned under fallen branches and forest debris than in any other type of boating accident. And Kal almost boosted those statistics. We rounded a blind bend and met a dam of warped, webbed spruce trunks. He tried to backpaddle, but the current was too strong. Then he tried to turn around, but he didn't have a real command of his strokes. The boat was swept sideways into the tangle.

Kal leaped from the boat not a second too soon—the kayak rolled upside-down and jammed, half-submerged, in the log pile—and struggled through a slalom of sticks and logs across the fast water to shore.

While Kal caught his breath and licked his wounds, Bart and Dick worked to free the wedged kayak. When it came loose, Kal declined to get back in and took his place on one of the rafts.

Late in the morning we sighted, along a granite face high above us, two flossy white mountain goats (actually they're related to an Asian antelope, believed to have migrated across a frozen Bering Strait millennia ago). Before we could get to our cameras, though, we were swept around the corner. And before we could tighten our life jackets, we were careening down an accelerating flume. The whole river was suddenly whipping along at 10 miles per hour or more. We were going faster than I had ever been in anything without an engine. Rolling velocity waves formed, and the wind that bit was strong. But what a joy! A boatman's dream: a river in which downstream strokes were not required. Almost every wild river run in the United States ends in a lake that nature did not create, and after an invigorating trip of playing in spritely rapids, the boatman more often than not has to put his or her back into a grueling pull across stagnant water, sometimes against upstream winds and between beer-can jetsam. But not here.

We continued to clip along at a giggling pace, stopping occasionally to hike to a waterfall or up a canyon. By evening we'd covered 30 miles and were at the confluence with the McConnell River, the Tat's largest tributary.

We had yet to get within 15 miles of a real glacier, but all around was evidence of their activity. Much of the riverbank was made up of glacial moraine, an accumulation of boulders, stones, and other debris carried and deposited by glaciers past. And of course, all the tributary canyons and valleys and the bizarre granite pinnacles and rock formations owed their existence to the glaciers' sculpturing prowess.

Evening was a long time coming. A few of us sat back and reflected on the fact that we were perhaps the first ever to "raft" the river—a dubious distinction, but one that gave us a certain degree of pride in being where we were at that time.

"It will probably be some time before another rafting party gets down here," someone observed.

I nodded in agreement and moved into Skip's tent to go over the maps, a nightly routine.

Fresh snow creamed the surrounding mountains the following morning, saber-toothed peaks that solemnly marched toward the horizon. Between the mountains glaciers hung like blue tongues, 14 within sight. A golden eagle soared and three sea gulls flapped above us.

That morning we scudded down the river at the usual freeway speed, but the adrenaline wasn't pumping quite so fast. We were getting used to the velocity. Until we hit what we would later name Moraine Maelstrom.

135

Continued on page 142.

136

During the August up-river spawning run the Tatshenshini is packed with chinook (king), sockeye, and coho salmon (left). *It is a challenge to make a catch, however, since they gorge themselves with seafood before hitting the fresh water so that they aren't bothered with eating, or tempted by bait, during their passage. Right: The Icefield Ranges along the river make up the world's largest nonpolar glacier system.*

Mark Jensen

137

Mark Jensen

138

Alsek Bay—rimmed with fireweed on one side and the seven-mile-wide face of the Alsek Glacier on the other. Ice chunks the size of buildings continually calve into the bay, creating tidal-like waves that can wipe out an ill-placed camp.

Pamela Roberson

140

Pamela Roberson

Pamela Robertson

The Tatshenshini is the ultimate ice river, where rafts share the currents with floating ice sculptures—slowly turning pieces of cracked glacier that float by like huge glittering jewels. The river itself is an unequaled gem, often called the most visually spectacular river in America.

Without warning the river screamed around a sharp bend and washed up onto a tilted flange of rock with water sculpted over it in a long, curling forelock that broke backward. Before we could react we were in it—a 50-yard stretch of crazy water: boils, whirlpools, hydraulics, and souse holes. The oars were useless. Body English was the only tool we could use to keep from flipping. When the boat bucked and keeled one way, we threw our weight the other way. We yawed and lurched and filled with water, and as suddenly as we were in it, we were out, bobbing in the eddy below.

All three boats (Dick had lashed his kayak atop one of the rafts) ran the gauntlet with the same results. We had to catch our breath after that one, so we pulled in below, built a fire, put on some coffee, and buzzed about the unexpected rapid. Until I looked up . . . at one of the most magnificent sights I had ever seen. The Melbern Glacier—the largest we'd seen yet and one that flows continuously over the ridge to the heart of Glacier Bay—was bathed in sunlight, reflecting a magical, prismatic glow. Probably at that very moment, scores of passengers on a Princess Cruise were at the other end of the glacier ogling back, equally awed.

That evening, to dress up the menu, Bart and I went hunting for natural edibles. We found sour grass, wild cucumbers (the size of peanuts), wild celery, and low-brush cranberries. Billy also went hunting and came back grinning and munching a juicy red berry. It wasn't readily recognizable, so Bart leafed through the guidebook and found it under the section on poisonous plants. It was something called baneberry. That put Billy in a foul mood, until we read in the fine print that it takes large doses of the berry to cause any adverse effects.

The following day the river started to braid. The braiding quickly got messier and messier, finally looking like the Medusa. It was impossible to tell which channel to take. Because we were still traveling along at a dizzying pace, we had to make split-second decisions. And more than once we'd choose what appeared to be the main channel only to find it dividing, then dividing again and then again. And we'd suddenly screech to a stop on a shoal, at which point we'd put on our wet-suit booties, get out, and push.

The scenery, though, was fuel enough to keep us going. On our right was the green, lushly forested, stark gray granite Noisy Range, while in almost blinding contrast the St. Elias Range loomed on our left in all its glacial glory.

Sometime in the afternoon of the seventh day, we merged with the Alsek River and were immediately floating in a glacial Mississippi. The silt was so thick that it created an almost deafening sound as it scratched the bottom of our boats, sounding like sand being poured down a tin slide. The banks of the river were a mile apart. So, instead of sailing down the center, where if a boat flipped no one would have a chance of swimming to shore, we hugged the left bank.

We didn't make it far, though, before a field of purple and red fireweed seemed to explode next to us. We had to pull over and camp. The backdrop was a series of glaciers that appeared to be only one or two miles away. Several of us tried to hike to the base of the closest, but after trodding a good six miles and finding ourselves not visibly closer to the glacier, we realized distances were deceptive in the great proportions of the St. Elias Range. Defeated, we turned to head back to camp. I took a step and the ground began to shake and grumble. I'd read that the southeastern Alaska and Canada strip was the most active seismic zone in North America, and I heard myself yell "Earthquake!" as I hit the dirt.

But no. Looking back I had time to see a sheet of ice chunks falling from the glacier, the vestiges of a much larger fall. Geology in action. And it was only the beginning. All that night the earth groaned and growled as glaciers moved and houses of ice calved off.

Alaska! The next day we officially crossed into the forty-ninth state and the Tongass National Forest. Again, we didn't get far. After an hour's floating, we came to a glacier that actually spilled into the river. No deceptive distances here. We moored to its base and took off on a glacier walk.

First, we had to scramble over scree and kame to the hard crystalline lip of the glacier. It was electric blue. It was eerie. Beneath us we could hear the sound of *moulin*—melted ice rushing through honeycombed chasms. We had to step slowly and gingerly along the glacier's wrinkled blue back, over crevasses and around grottos. One slip and you could disappear down a bottomless hole that might close instantly with the shifting ice, grinding your bones into silt and your flesh, eventually, into salmon eggs.

The next day, for the first time, bad weather cuffed us. The wind howled. It rained. And we shivered. So, after just six miles we decided to set up camp, across from the Novatak Glacier, to wait out the brooding weather. The day was spent playing chess, reading, and writing in our journals. By dusk the clouds were dissipating, and the sunset panorama seemed otherworldly. The river appeared as a long, coiling image of light, a chill, bending flame. All the colors and tones seemed reversed and exaggerated, something like a two-color negative. My eyes couldn't understand or assimilate the scene.

Sunday brought us to the crème de la crème of glaciers—the Alsek, with its seven-mile-wide face pouring right into a bay annexed to the river. Ice chunks the size of towns were almost constantly cracking off the face and crashing into the glassy water. About 500 yards back we made camp—far enough to be out of danger, but close enough to watch. Each time a major piece fell, about once an hour, it sounded as if the sky were falling and the ground trembled like jelly. What happened to these massive ice chunks after collapsing into the water? We couldn't really tell from where we were, but it looked as if they collected downstream in an ice-floe log-jam, which could prove troublesome.

We would worry about that later, however. The sun was smiling, the clouds were on the lam. It was a perfect day for a hike. First, we wandered over to the edge of the molten lead–colored lagoon at the foot of the Alsek Glacier, scaring a black bear from his fishing spot along the way. We sat down on a driftwood pile and gazed across at the voluptuous curves of the Deception Hills and, beyond them, the glacier snaking down from the ice fields that disappear into the sky. In the foreground a freshly cut iceberg floated just 30 yards offshore, directly in front of our perch. Its resemblance to a submarine, both in shape and size, was uncanny, and no sooner had we christened it the *Nautilus* than it was torpedoed, or so it seemed. Without warning, a several-ton piece broke off the stern bridge and plopped into the water, leaving the main body rocking and reeling until it actually rolled over and sank.

The fantastic was beginning to be the norm on this trip, so much so we almost expected each day to bring something better. And that night we weren't disappointed. The northern lights or aurora borealis appeared for the first time back upriver over the Novatak Glacier. It began as a pulsating green fanning across the firmament. Then it grew in intensity and variety, until spears of light from both ends of the spectrum flashed across the horizon in seemingly syncopated rhythm.

The morning was clear. To the south, Mount Fairweather, which had been eluding us until now, presented its 15,300-foot crown. Most of the peaks around us capped off at 8,000 feet, so the spectacle of seeing for the first time a mountain twice as high as the rim of the Grand Canyon when looking up from river level was impressive indeed.

August 24—my birthday. And I couldn't think of a better place to be. We celebrated with some cinnamon sweet rolls that Doug baked from scratch in the Dutch oven, and Dick fired off a few rounds of the now legally unsealed .357 MAGNUM®. Then, downstream for the last lap. Two miles after camp we came to Gateway Knob, a promontory island at the mouth of the Alsek Glacier lagoon. Ninety-five percent of the river rushed to the left of the island, and a trickle eased down the right. We were almost swept down the left, but the passage looked as though it might be clogged with ice chunks from the glacier. The right passage, however, presented an unquestionably clear course. So, we bent the oars and pulled like mules out of the current over to the right channel where we shoaled several times and had to get out to push. But we made it around the Knob.

It was the correct maneuver. Once beyond the Knob, we looked back upstream to see the road not taken. It was completely barricaded with ice. The water crashed into the rampart, then burrowed into its subsurface core, where it flowed through ice caverns in a frenzy. It was a Channel of Death. We wouldn't have had a prayer. Our right choice was a wonderful birthday present.

As we merged with the water that had taken the other course, we also joined hundreds of ice floes of every conceivable shape and size that had broken from the barricade. Now the river was an obstacle course. We wove through the maze of shimmering ice flotsam, always avoiding the hotel-sized chunks that were continually crumbling. We were doing fine, too, until we hit the rapids.

The last rapids before Dry Bay were a series of convergence waves, easily navigated under usual circumstances. But the ice made it all a bit more sporting. There was no way to brake as we entered the tongue, so we had to rely on ferrying capabilities to dodge ice entering with us. It was impossible, though. One jagged Chevy-shaped piece seemed to be charging us, and it was gaining. We outmaneuvered it through the worst of the waves, but it made a last lunge for us as the rapid was slowing and rammed our rear. Amazingly, we didn't puncture. The ludicrousness of it all struck me. Instead of battling traffic on the Santa Monica Freeway, I was battling car-sized ice cubes on the Tatshenshini Throughway, and I'd just been in a fender bender in a bottleneck.

On the final bend we saw our last grizzly, scooping up maybe a fifth of the 100 pounds of salmon he eats in a day. Then, we were at the Dry Bay Fishing Company, an isolated five-person netting and cleaning operation, the only outpost of civilization for 50 miles in any direction. It was also the terminus for our expedition.

As we disassembled the frames and sorted the gear, the sun peeked out, immediately warming the air. I took off my shirt and let the Alaskan sun kindle my skin. Then as we began to load the six-seater Cessna that would take us back to civilization, a tube of fog drifted in, the clouds coiled back over the sun, and the temperature plunged. But I kept my shirt off and it stayed off for the rest of the loading, even as a drizzle misted the air and the thermometer showed close to freezing. I was still warm, as warm as I had ever been on a river trip. The Tatshenshini had made me warm, a warmth that stays with me still.

Whitewater Lore

Glossary

Backboil: At the bottom of a rapid, fast water meets calm water and washes back upstream on each side of the rapid. The fast water moves back in a curling pattern that creates complex cross currents that boil up and burst through the surface of the river. A backboil is in the backeddy.

Braid: When a river interweaves between islands and shoals, creating different channels.

Broaching: When a boat runs sideways to the current or is pinned perpendicular to an obstacle in the river.

Catch a crab: When an oar hits an eddy, a tricky current, or an underwater object and is jerked out of control, as if a crab had gotten hold of it.

Convergence waves: Also known as velocity waves, they are created when fast-flowing water in a wide river is constricted because the river narrows suddenly. The constriction causes waves to bulge up in the center of the river.

Cusecs: Cubic feet per second. The volume of a river flowing past a single point.

Endo: To turn end over end.

Hairball: Risky.

Haystack: A pyramid-shaped standing wave caused by deceleration of current from underwater resistance.

Hydraulic: The effect created when water flows over a ledge, dam, weir, or steep drop and its base curls back on itself forming a strong reverse rolling stationary wave.

Interference waves: Like convergence waves, except that instead of both sides of the river narrowing, the river is interrupted on one side by a tributary canyon that floods and washes debris into the river, constricting the flow of water. The sudden constriction causes the interference waves.

Pour-over: A rock or boulder that water washes over, creating a hole behind.

Souse hole: A large hydraulic hole that exists behind a rock that is barely below the surface of the water. The water dynamics creates a vacuum behind the rock, and there is often a flow of water over the rock, enabling a raft to float over it and drop into the hole.

Stubblefield: A passage of water filled with so many rocks that you can stub the boat on them.

Tongue: The slick glossy V of quiet water that marks the entrance to a rapid.

Tubestand: A raft turns perpendicular to the water and stands on its side tube.

Wrapping: When a raft wraps against a rock and is held in place by the current.

National Wild and Scenic River System

In 1968, the U.S. government created the National Wild and Scenic River System to provide federal protection for rivers in much the same way that parklands are protected. The rivers are selected on the basis of certain criteria—such as their scenic, recreational, geologic, historic, and cultural value and their fish and wildlife populations. Once chosen, the rivers are protected from dams, diversion projects, and riverside development that would alter their character. The first eight rivers designated as part of this system are known as the Instant 8. The Rogue in Oregon and the Middle Fork of the Salmon in Idaho are among those eight.

River Classification System
Based on the American Whitewater Association's system.

Class I: Easy rapids with small waves, clear passages.

Class II: Rapids of moderate difficulty, clear passages; maneuvering necessary.

Class III: Numerous waves, some rocks and eddies; passages narrow but clear.

Class IV: Long rapids with powerful, irregular waves and dangerous rocks. Scouting mandatory on first passage.

Class V: Extremely difficult, long and violent rapids with little room for recovery. Obstructed passages, powerful current, steep gradient; close study required before each run. Requires considerable experience and skill. All possible precautions must be taken.

Class VI: Difficulties of Class V carried to extreme. Nearly impossible and very dangerous. For experts only, at favorable water levels and with all precautions.

Whitewater Adventure was produced in association with the publisher by McQuiston & Partners in Del Mar, California: art direction, Don McQuiston; editorial direction, Tom Chapman; design and production supervision, Joyce Sweet; mechanical production, Kristi Mendola; map design and production, Patti Judd; production coordination, Marci Wellens; copyediting, Robin Witkin; composition, TypeLink; text type, Goudy Old Style; printed and bound in Japan by Dai Nippon Printing Company, Ltd.

144

7-Day

917   Bangs, Richard, 1950-
BAN   Whitewater adventure.

        WITHDRAWN

$40.00   4/18/91

© THE BAKER & TAYLOR CO.